LYNYRD SKYNYRD

EASY GUITAR WITH RIFFS AND SOLOS

Cover photo courtesy: MICHAEL OCHS ARCHIVES.COM

ISBN: 978-0-634-06712-9

HAL•LEONARD®
CORPORATION

7777 W. BLUEMOUND RD. P.O. BOX 13819 MILWAUKEE, WI 53213

Visit Hal Leonard Online at
www.HalLeonard.com

STRUM AND PICK PATTERNS

This chart contains the suggested strum and pick patterns that are referred to by number at the beginning of each song in this book. The symbols ⊓ and ∨ in the strum patterns refer to down and up strokes, respectively. The letters in the pick patterns indicate which right-hand fingers plays which strings.

p = thumb
i = index finger
m = middle finger
a = ring finger

For example; Pick Pattern 2
is played: thumb - index - middle - ring

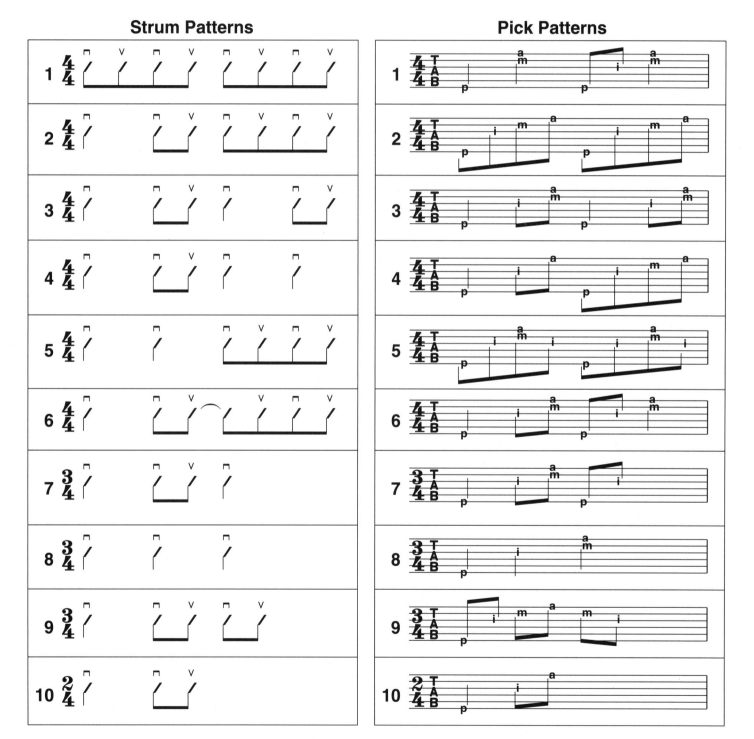

You can use the 3/4 Strum or Pick Patterns in songs written in compound meter (6/8, 9/8, 12/8, etc.).
For example, you can accompany a song in 6/8 by playing the 3/4 pattern twice in each measure.
The 4/4 Strum and Pick Patterns can be used for songs written in cut time (¢) by doubling the note
time values in the patterns. Each pattern would therefore last two measures in cut time.

Guitar Notation Legend

Guitar Music can be notated three different ways: on a *musical staff*, in *tablature*, and in *rhythm slashes*.

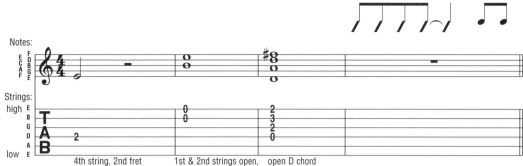

RHYTHM SLASHES are written above the staff. Strum chords in the rhythm indicated. Use the chord diagrams found at the top of the first page of the transcription for the appropriate chord voicings. Round noteheads indicate single notes.

THE MUSICAL STAFF shows pitches and rhythms and is divided by bar lines into measures. Pitches are named after the first seven letters of the alphabet.

TABLATURE graphically represents the guitar fingerboard. Each horizontal line represents a string, and each number represents a fret.

HALF-STEP BEND: Strike the note and bend up 1/2 step.

WHOLE-STEP BEND: Strike the note and bend up one step.

GRACE NOTE BEND: Strike the note and immediately bend up as indicated.

SLIGHT (MICROTONE) BEND: Strike the note and bend up 1/4 step.

BEND AND RELEASE: Strike the note and bend up as indicated, then release back to the original note. Only the first note is struck.

PRE-BEND: Bend the note as indicated, then strike it.

VIBRATO: The string is vibrated by rapidly bending and releasing the note with the fretting hand.

WIDE VIBRATO: The pitch is varied to a greater degree by vibrating with the fretting hand.

HAMMER-ON: Strike the first (lower) note with one finger, then sound the higher note (on the same string) with another finger by fretting it without picking.

PULL-OFF: Place both fingers on the notes to be sounded. Strike the first note and without picking, pull the finger off to sound the second (lower) note.

LEGATO SLIDE: Strike the first note and then slide the same fret-hand finger up or down to the second note. The second note is not struck.

SHIFT SLIDE: Same as legato slide, except the second note is struck.

TRILL: Very rapidly alternate between the notes indicated by continuously hammering on and pulling off.

TAPPING: Hammer ("tap") the fret indicated with the pick-hand index or middle finger and pull off to the note fretted by the fret hand.

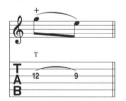

NATURAL HARMONIC: Strike the note while the fret-hand lightly touches the string directly over the fret indicated.

PINCH HARMONIC: The note is fretted normally and a harmonic is produced by adding the edge of the thumb or the tip of the index finger of the pick hand to the normal pick attack.

PICK SCRAPE: The edge of the pick is rubbed down (or up) the string, producing a scratchy sound.

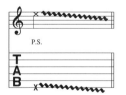

MUFFLED STRINGS: A percussive sound is produced by laying the fret hand across the string(s) without depressing, and striking them with the pick hand.

PALM MUTING: The note is partially muted by the pick hand lightly touching the string(s) just before the bridge.

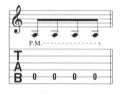

RAKE: Drag the pick across the strings indicated with a single motion.

TREMOLO PICKING: The note is picked as rapidly and continuously as possible.

VIBRATO BAR DIVE AND RETURN: The pitch of the note or chord is dropped a specified number of steps (in rhythm) then returned to the original pitch.

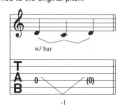

VIBRATO BAR SCOOP: Depress the bar just before striking the note, then quickly release the bar.

VIBRATO BAR DIP: Strike the note and then immediately drop a specified number of steps, then release back to the original pitch.

3

Call Me the Breeze

Words and Music by John Cale

Intro
Moderately

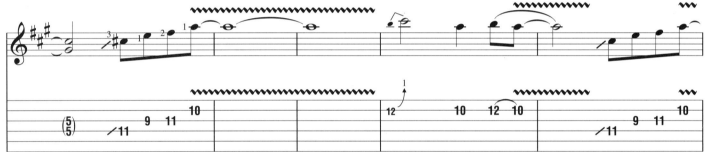

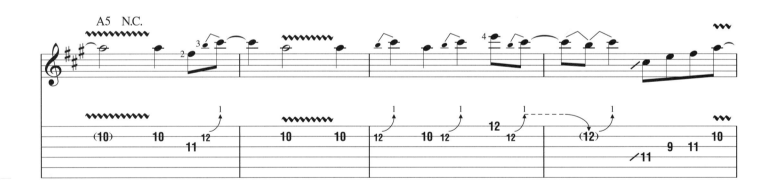

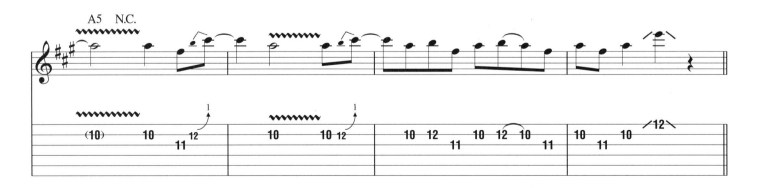

Strum Pattern: 3, 4
Pick Pattern: 3, 4

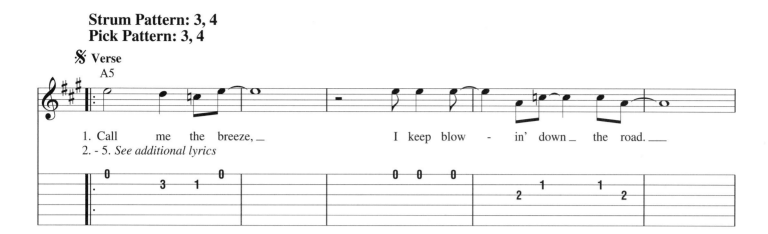

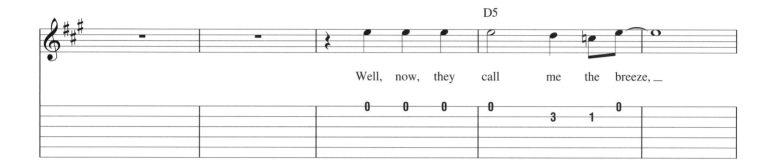

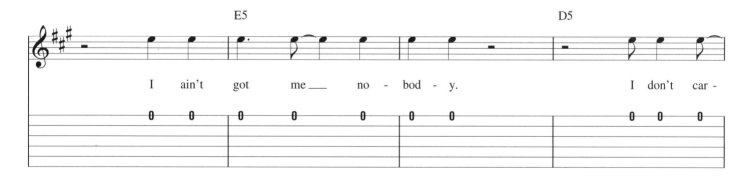

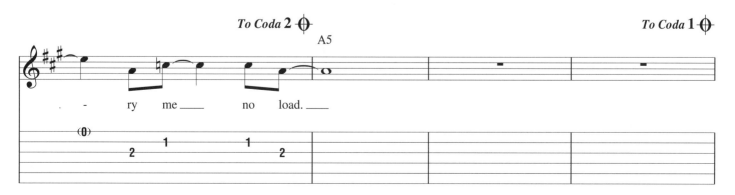

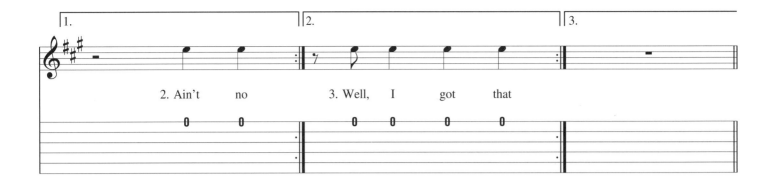

2. Ain't no   3. Well, I   got   that

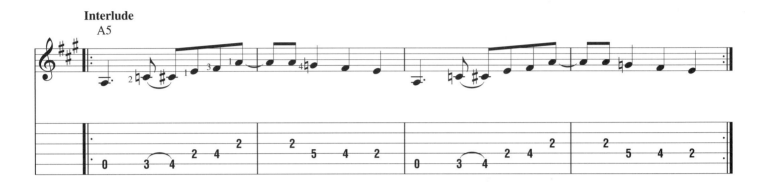

Interlude

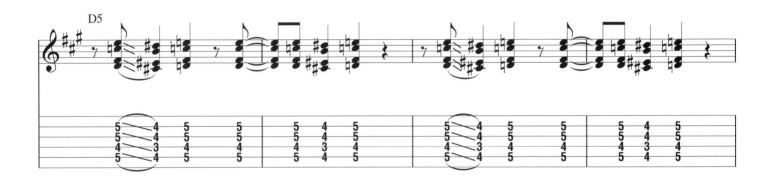

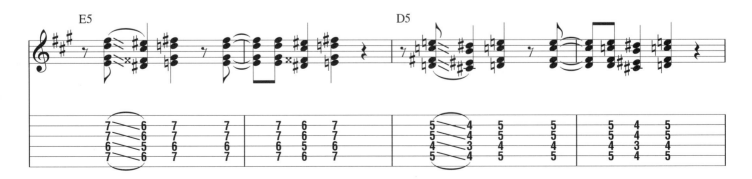

4. Well, I

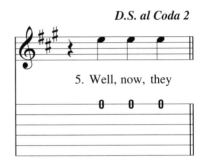

⊕ Coda 1   ⊕ Coda 2

D.S. al Coda 2

5. Well, now, they

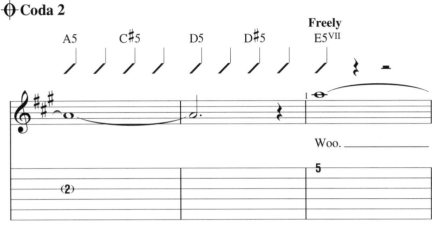

Woo.

Spoken: Mister Breeze.

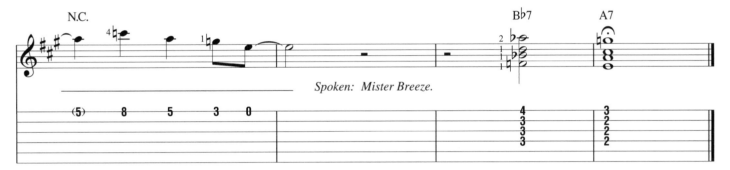

Additional Lyrics

2. Ain't no change in the weather,
   Ain't no changes in me.
   Well, there ain't no change in the weather,
   Ain't no changes in me.
   And I ain't hidin' from nobody,
   Nobody's hidin' from me.
Spoken: Oh, that's the way it's s'posed to be.

3. Well, I got that green light, baby,
   I got to keep movin' on.
   Well, I got that green light, babe,
   I got to keep movin' on.
   Well, I might go out to California,
   Might go down to Georgia, I don't know.

4. Well, I dig you Georgia peaches,
   Makes me feel right at home.
   Well, now, I dig you Georgia peaches,
   Makes me feel right at home.
   But I don't love me no one woman,
   So I can't stay in Georgia long.

5. Well, now, they call me the breeze,
   I keep blowin' down the road.
   Well, now, they call me the breeze,
   I keep blowin' down the road.
   I ain't got me nobody,
   I don't carry me no load.

Don't Ask Me No Questions

Words and Music by Ronnie Van Zant and Gary Rossington

Strum Pattern: 2, 3
Pick Pattern: 4

Intro
Moderately

*Slide gtr. arr. for gtr.

% Verse

1. Well,   ev-'ry time that I come home, no-
2., 3. *See additional lyrics*

bod - y wants to let me be. ___   It seems that all the   friends I've got ___ just

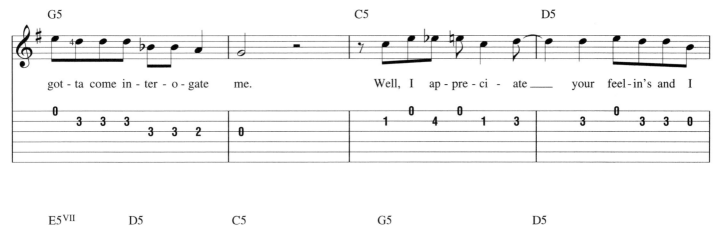

gotta come in-ter-o-gate me. Well, I ap-pre-ci-ate ___ your feel-in's and I

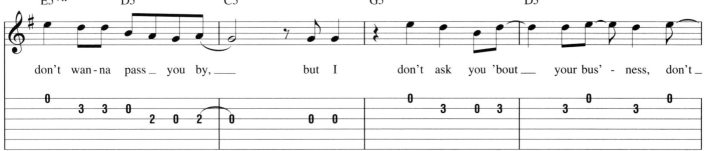

don't wan-na pass ___ you by, ___ but I don't ask you 'bout ___ your bus' - ness, don't ___

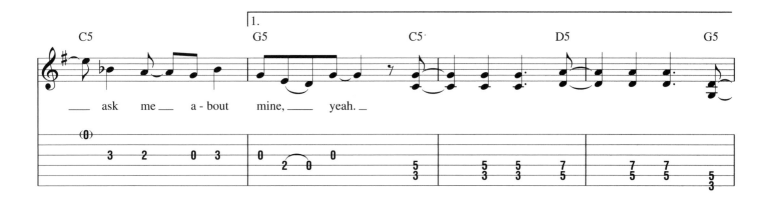

___ ask me ___ a - bout mine, ___ yeah. ___

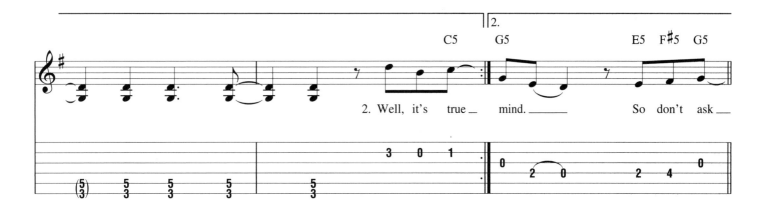

2. Well, it's true ___ mind. ___ So don't ask ___

Chorus

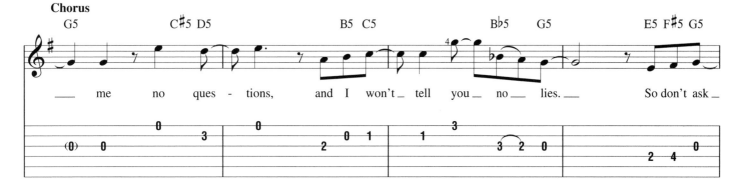

___ me no ques - tions, and I won't ___ tell you ___ no ___ lies. So don't ask ___

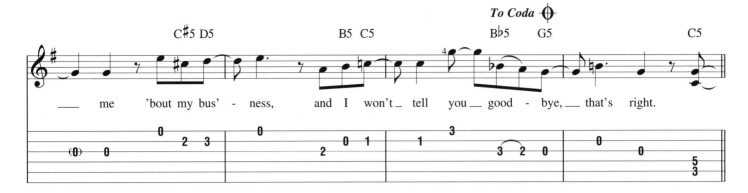

To Coda ⊕

C#5 D5   B5 C5   B♭5 G5   C5

_ me 'bout my bus' - ness,   and I won't _ tell you _ good - bye, _ that's right.

Interlude

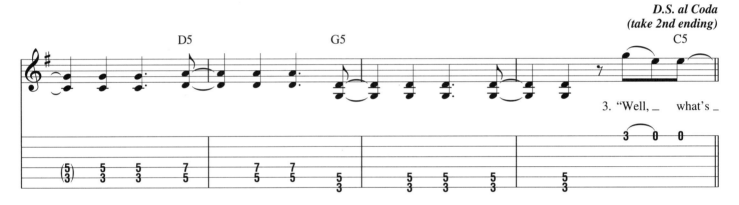

C5   D5   G5   C5

Play 3 times

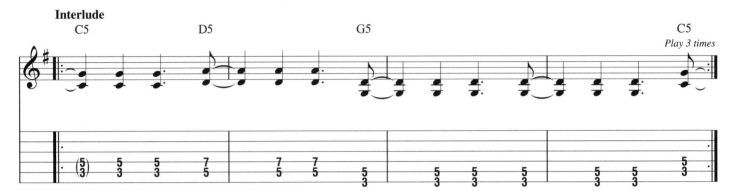

D.S. al Coda
(take 2nd ending)

D5   G5   C5

3. "Well, _ what's _

⊕ **Coda**

Chorus

E5 F#5 G5   C#5 D5   B5 C5

_ I said, don't ask _ no stu - pid ques - tions, and I won't

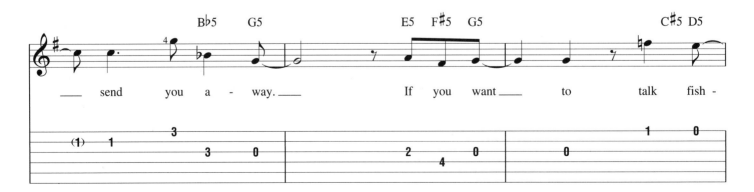

B♭5   G5   E5 F#5 G5   C#5 D5

_ send you a - way. _ If you want _ to talk fish -

-in', Well, I guess ___ that-'ll be o-kay. ___ *Spoken:* *What'd I say, huh?*

Outro

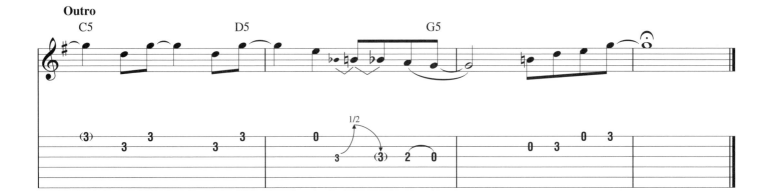

Additional Lyrics

2. Well, it's true, I love the money,
   And I love my brand new car.
   I like drinkin' the best of whiskey
   And playin' in a honky-tonk bar.
   But when I come off the road,
   Well, I just gotta have my time,
   'Cause I got to find a break in this action,
   Else I'm gonna lose my mind.

3. "Well, what's your favorite color and
   Do you dig the brothers?" It's drivin' me up the wall.
   And every time I think I can sleep
   Some fool has got to call.
   Well, don't you think that when I come home
   I just want a little peace of mind?
   If you wanna talk about the business,
   Buddy, you're just wastin' time.

Down South Jukin'

Words and Music by Ronnie Van Zant and Gary Rossington

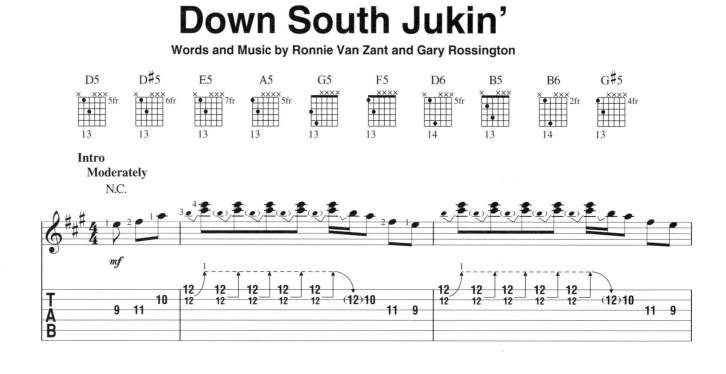

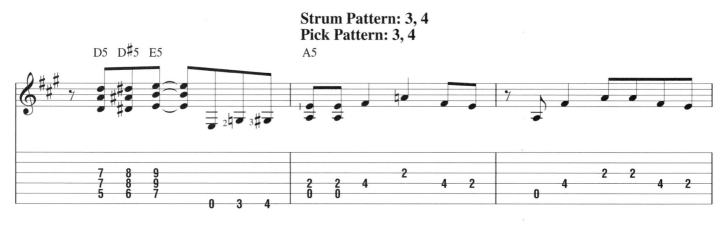

Strum Pattern: 3, 4
Pick Pattern: 3, 4

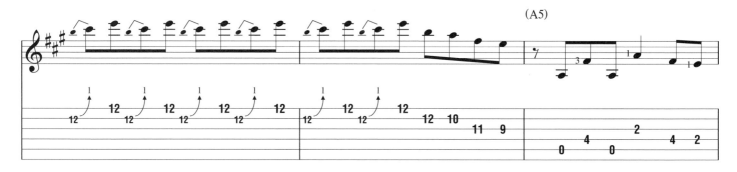

1. Well, ol' Bil-ly Joe told me said, "A
2., 3. *See additional lyrics*

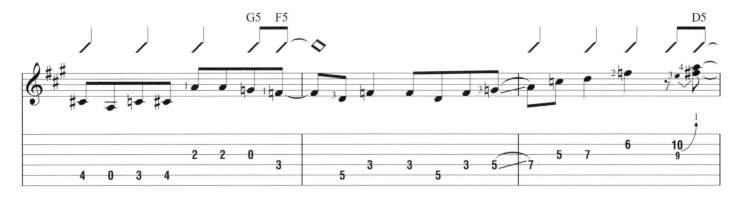

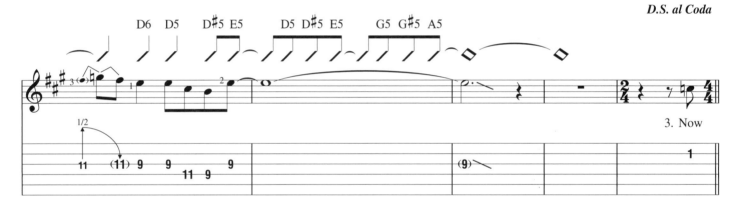

*Roll finger

D.S. al Coda

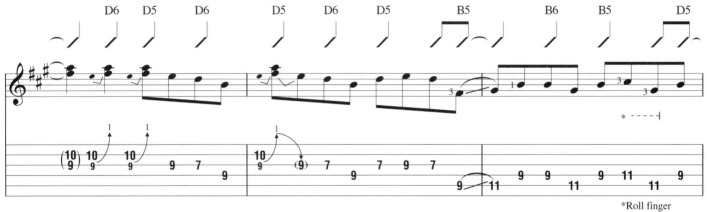

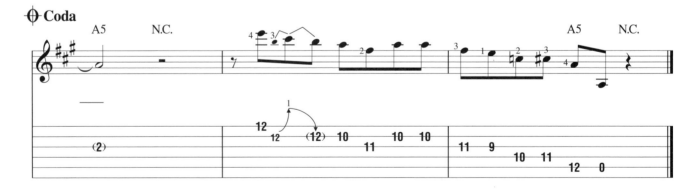

Additional Lyrics

2. Now put your Sunday pants on, let's a get out on the road.
   We been workin' all week and I think it's time we let go.
   He got a three fat mamas sittin' all alone.
   Gonna sip our wine, Lord, get it on.
   And do some down south jukin', lookin' for peace of mind.

3. Now come Monday morn' we'll be headed back to the field.
   And we'll be doin' our thing for poppin' all the beer.
   We'll overcome Friday night when we head to town,
   Tryin' to pick up any woman hangin' around.
   Do some down south jukin', lookin' for peace of mind.

Free Bird

Words and Music by Allen Collins and Ronnie Van Zant

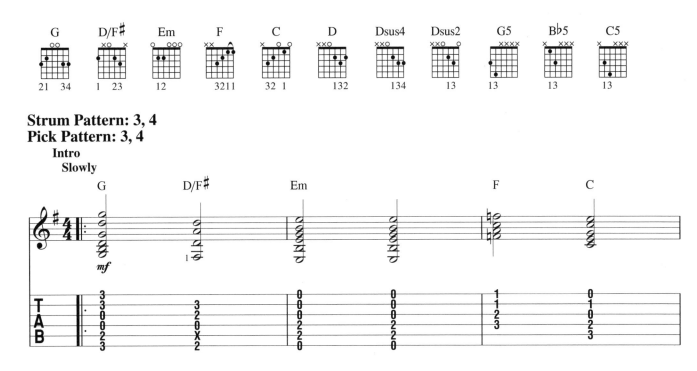

Strum Pattern: 3, 4
Pick Pattern: 3, 4

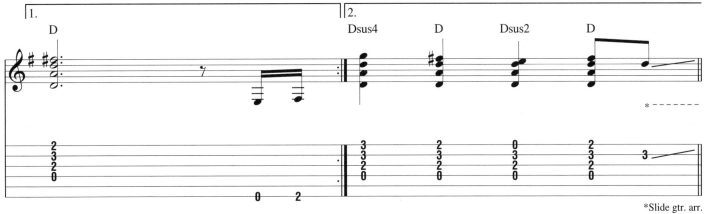

*Slide gtr. arr.
for gtr.

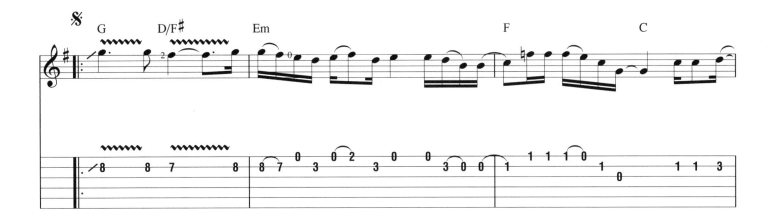

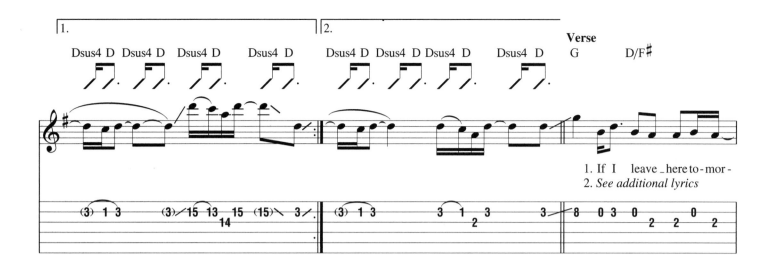

1. If I leave _ here to-mor-
2. *See additional lyrics*

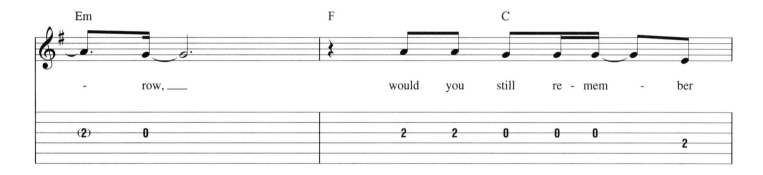

- row, ___ would you still re - mem - ber

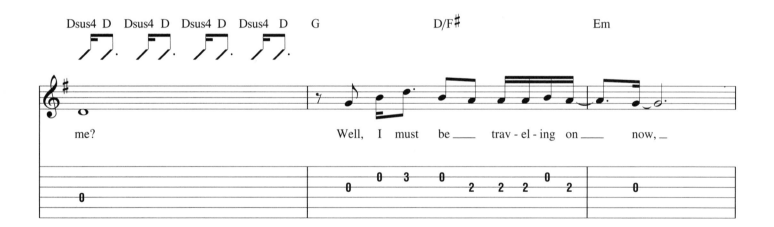

me? Well, I must be ___ trav - el - ing on ___ now, _

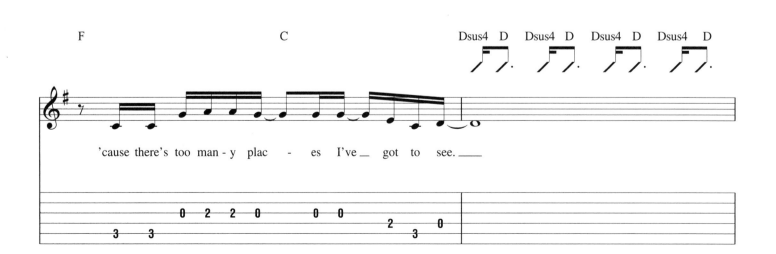

'cause there's too man - y plac - es I've _ got to see. ___

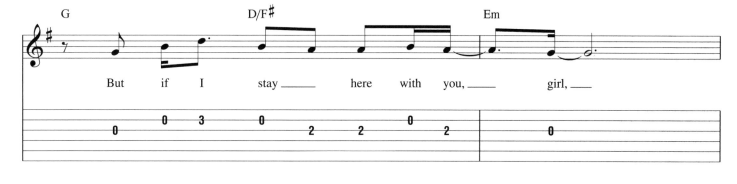

But if I stay ____ here with you, ____ girl, ____

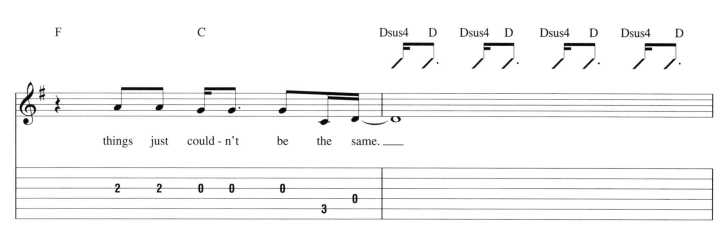

things just could-n't be the same. ____

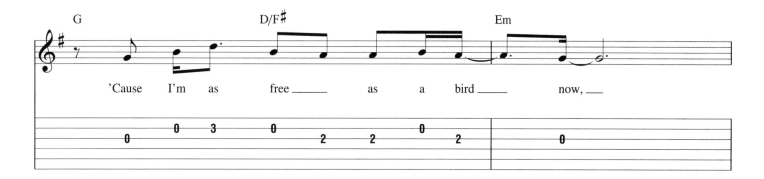

'Cause I'm as free ____ as a bird ____ now, ____

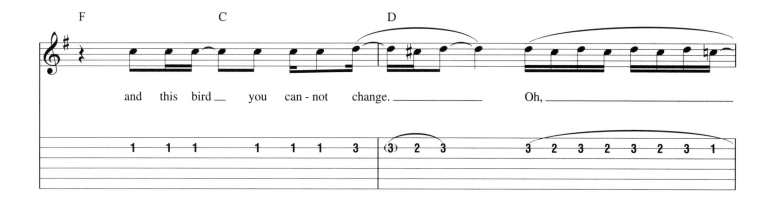

and this bird ____ you can-not change. ____ Oh, ____

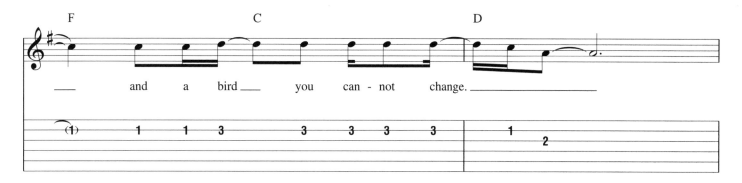

____ and a bird ____ you can-not change. ____

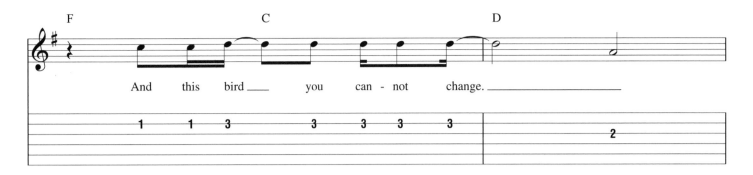

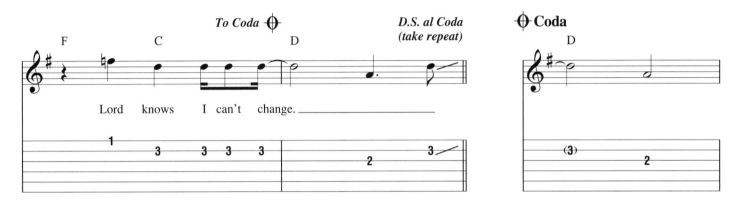

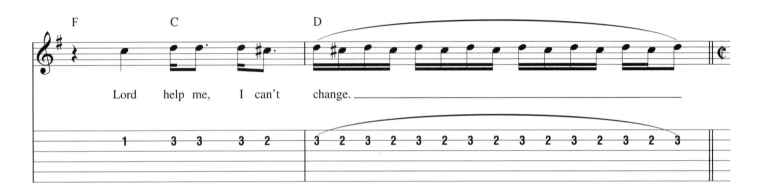

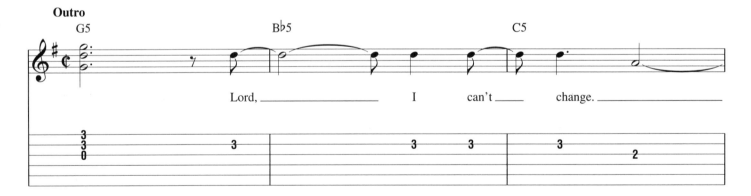

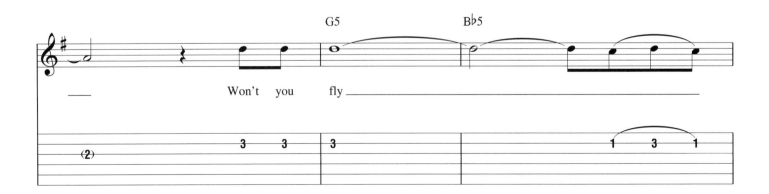

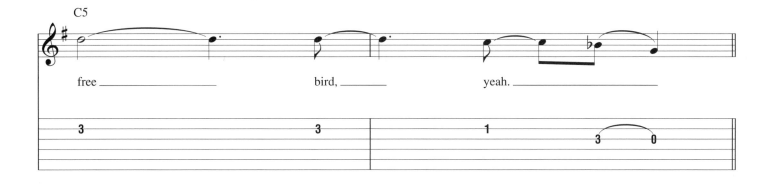

free _____ bird, _____ yeah. _____

Guitar Solo

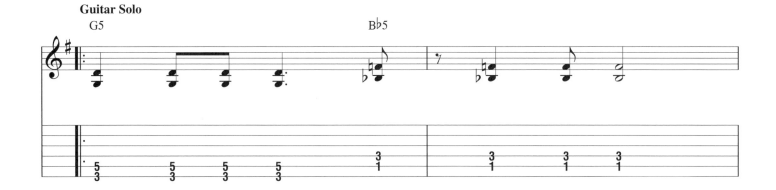

Repeat and fade

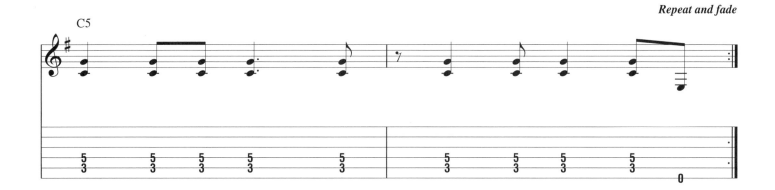

Additional Lyrics

2. Bye bye, baby, it's been sweet now, yeah, yeah.
   Though this feelin' I can't change.
   A please don't take it so badly,
   'Cause Lord knows I'm to blame.
   But if I stay here with you, girl,
   Things just couldn't be the same.
   'Cause I'm as free as a bird now,
   And this bird you cannot change.
   Oh, and a bird you cannot change.
   And this bird you cannot change.
   Lord knows I can't change.
   Lord help me, I can't change.

Gimme Back My Bullets

Words and Music by Gary Rossington and Ronnie Van Zant

*Muffle strings: A percussive sound is produced by laying the fret hand
across the strings without depressing, and striking them with the pick hand.

Strum Pattern: 3, 4
Pick Pattern: 4, 5

1. Life is so strange when it's
2., 3. *See additional lyrics*

chang - in', yes in - deed. Well, I've seen the hard times and the

pres - sure has been on me. But I keep on a work - in' like a

work - in' man do. _____ And I've got my act to - geth - er, gon - na

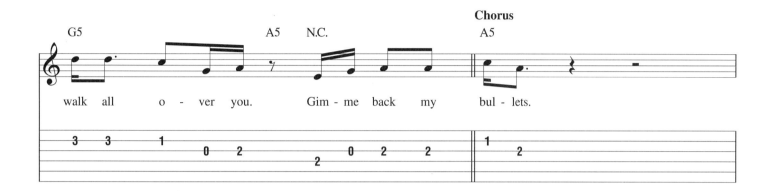

Chorus

walk all o - ver you. Gim - me back my bul - lets.

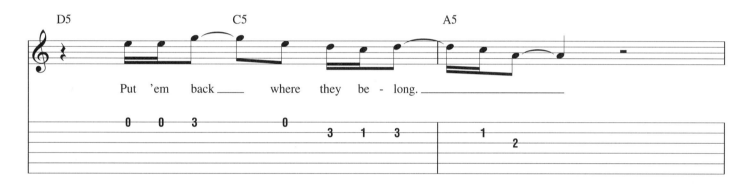

Put 'em back _____ where they be - long. _____

Ain't fool - in' a - round 'cause I've done had my fun. ____ Ain't gon - na see ____ no ____

1.

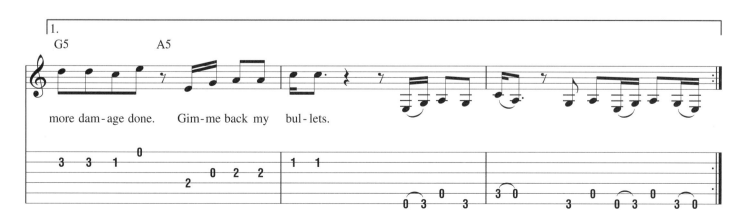

more dam - age done. Gim-me back my bul - lets.

2.

G5   N.C.(A5)   A5

more dam-age done.   Gim-me back,   gim-me back my   bul-lets.

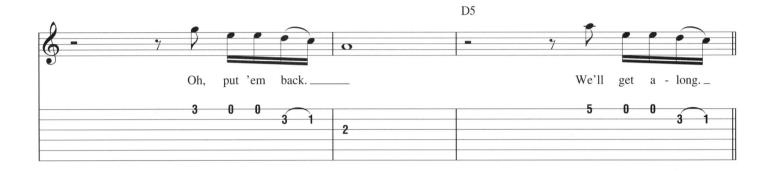

D5

Oh, put 'em back. _____   We'll get a-long. _____

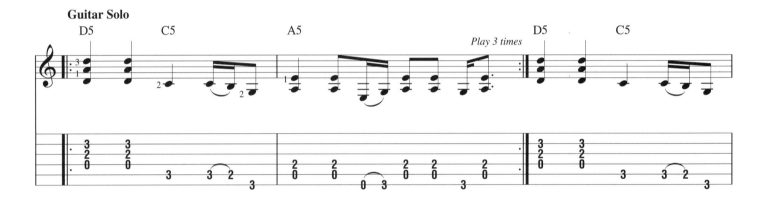

Guitar Solo

D5   C5   A5   *Play 3 times*   D5   C5

D.S. al Coda
(take 2nd ending)

A5   N.C.

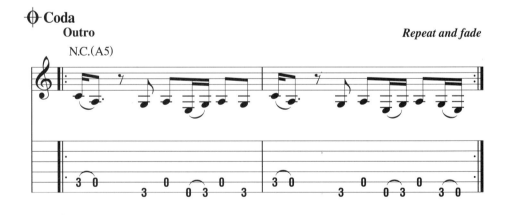

⊕ **Coda**
Outro   *Repeat and fade*

N.C.(A5)

Additional Lyrics

2. Sweet talkin' people done ran me outta town.
   And I've drank enough whiskey to float a battleship around.
   But I'm leavin' this game one step ahead of you.
   And you will not hear me cry, 'cause I do not sing the blues.

3. Been up and down since I turned seventeen.
   Well, I've been on top and then it seemed I lost the dream.
   But I've got it back, I'm feelin' better every day.
   Tell all those pencil pushers better get outta my way.

Gimme Three Steps

Words and Music by Allen Collins and Ronnie Van Zant

Strum Pattern: 5

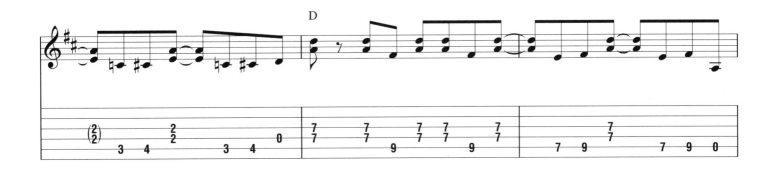

*T = Thumb on 6th string

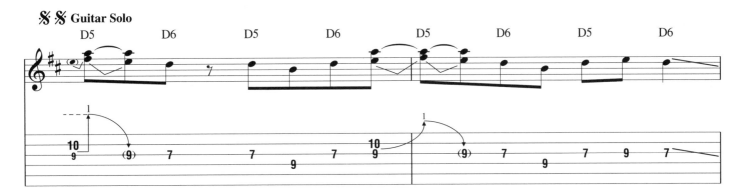

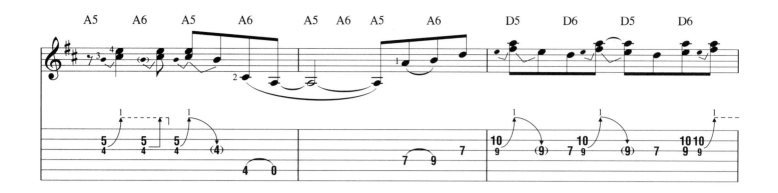

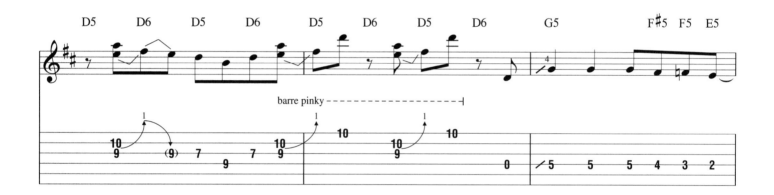

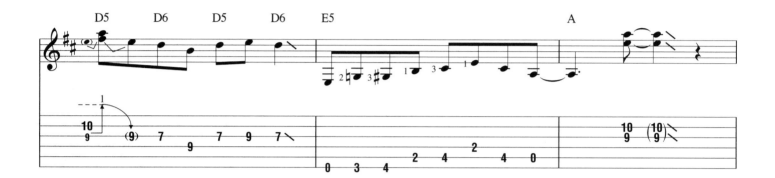

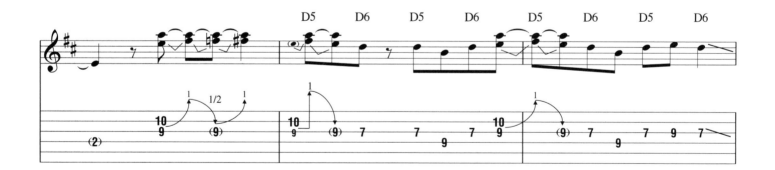

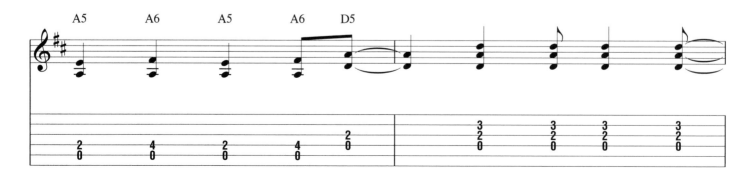

%. Verse

1. I was cut - tin' the rug __ down at a place called The Jug __ with a
2., 3. *See additional lyrics*

girl named __ Lin - da Lu, __ when a in walked a man __ with a

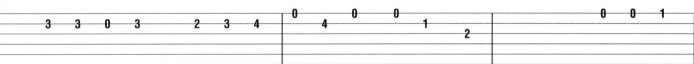

gun in his hand __ and he was look - in' for you know who. __ He said, "Hey, __

__ there fel - low with the hair col - ored yel - low, what you try - in' to prove? __

To Coda 1 ⊕

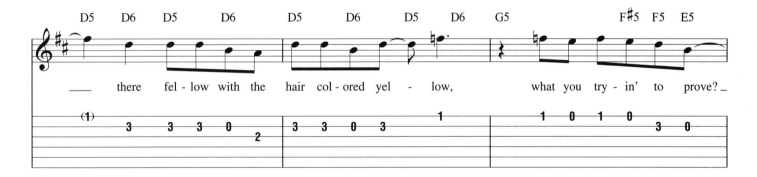

__ 'Cause that's my wom - an there, __ and I'm a man who __ cares, __ and this

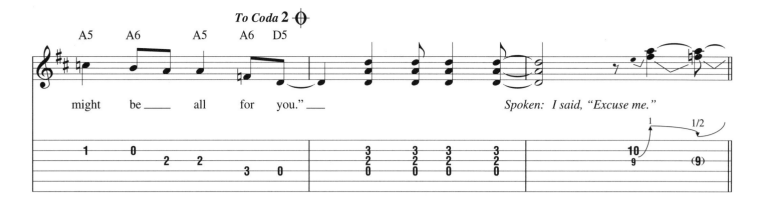

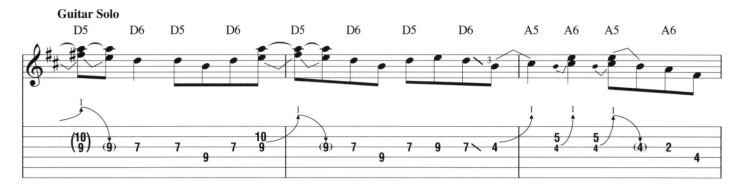

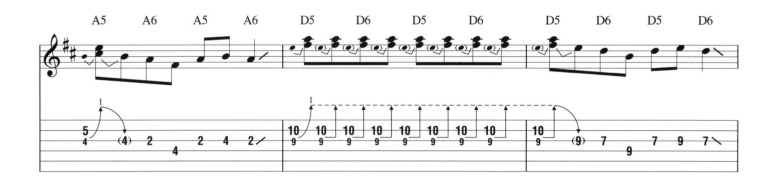

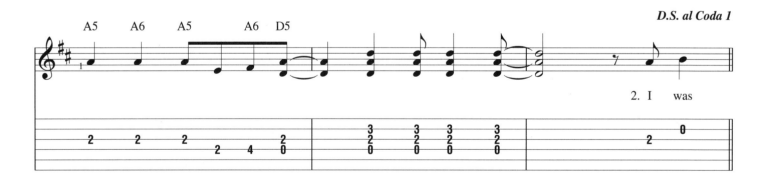

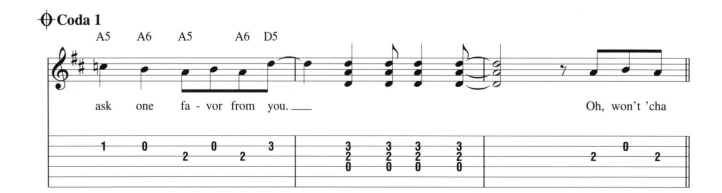

Chorus

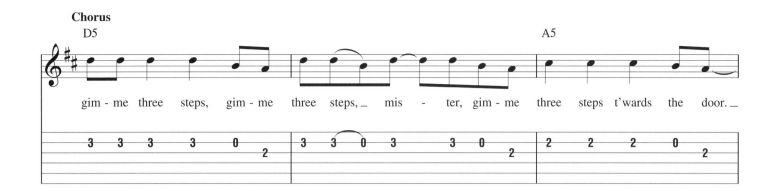

gim - me three steps, gim - me three steps, _ mis - ter, gim - me three steps t'wards the door. _

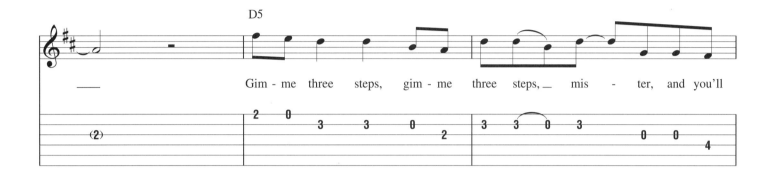

___ Gim - me three steps, gim - me three steps, _ mis - ter, and you'll

nev - er see a me no more. ___ *Spoken: For sure.*

Guitar Solo

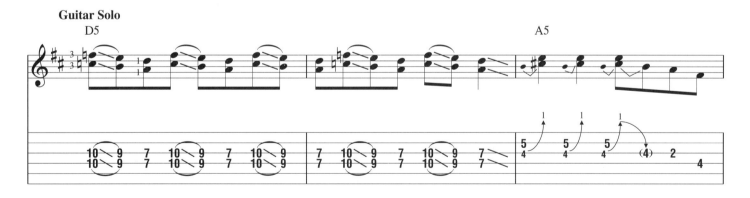

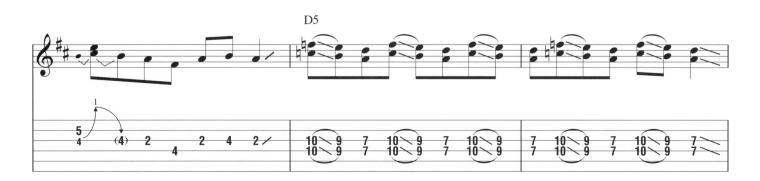

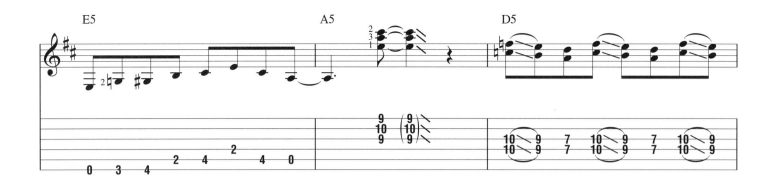

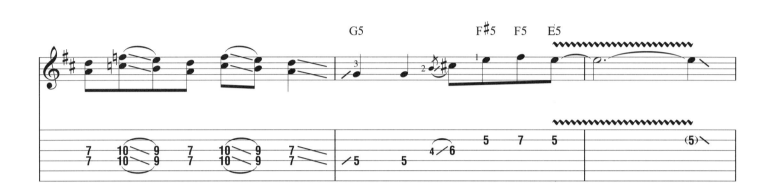

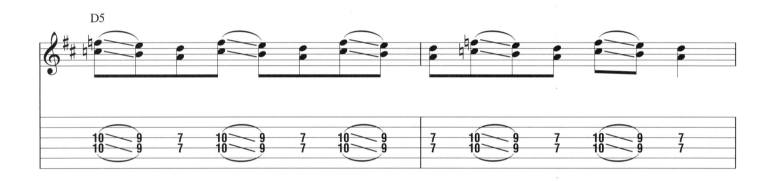

D.S. al Coda 2

3. Well, the

 Coda 2

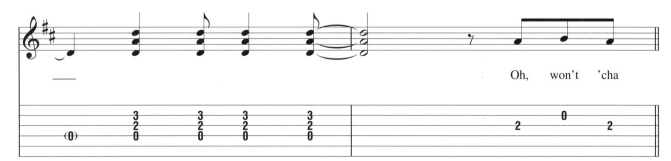

Oh, won't 'cha

Chorus

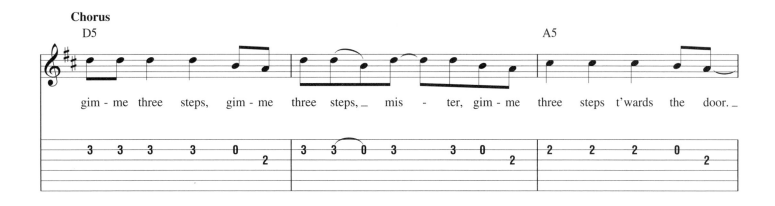

gim - me three steps, gim - me three steps, _ mis - ter, gim - me three steps t'wards the door. _

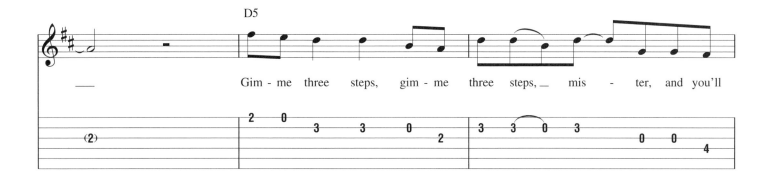

_ Gim - me three steps, gim - me three steps, _ mis - ter, and you'll

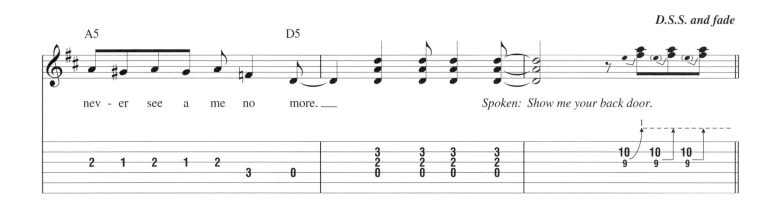

D.S.S. and fade

nev - er see a me no more. _ *Spoken: Show me your back door.*

Additional Lyrics

2. I was scared and fearin' for my life,
   I was shakin' like a leaf on a tree.
   'Cause he was lean and mean and big and bad, Lord,
   And pointin' that gun at me.
   Oh, wait a minute mister, I didn't even kiss her.
   Don't want no trouble with you.
   And I know you don't owe me but I wish you would let me
   Ask one favor from you.

3. Well, the crowd cleared away and I began to pray
   And the water fell on the floor.
   And I'm tellin' you son, well, it ain't no fun
   Starin' straight down a forty-four.
   Well, he turned and screamed at Linda Lu,
   And that's the break I was lookin' for.
   And you could hear me screamin' a mile away
   As I was headed out t'wards the door.

I Know a Little

Words and Music by Steve Earl Gaines

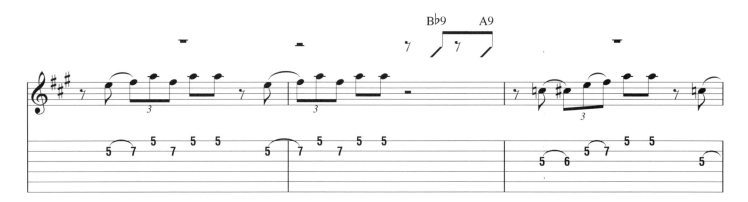

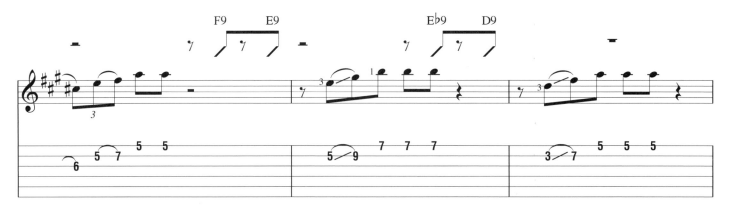

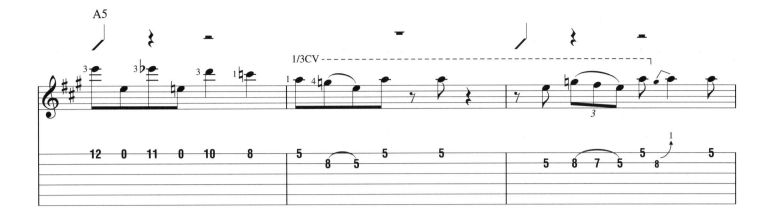

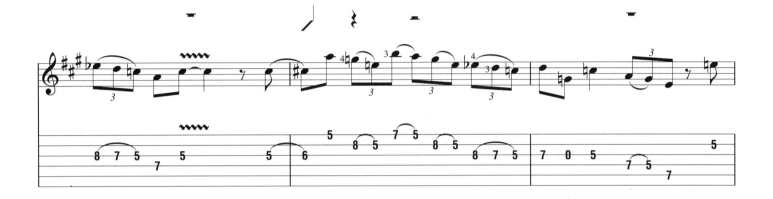

Strum Pattern: 4
Pick Pattern: 4

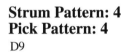

Spoken: Yes,   *sir.*

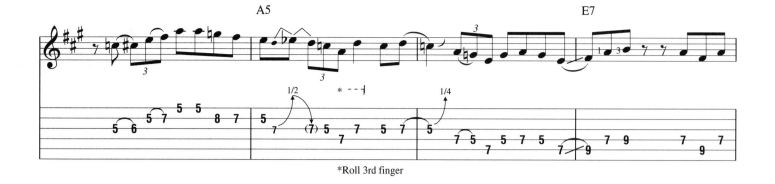

A5   E7

*Roll 3rd finger

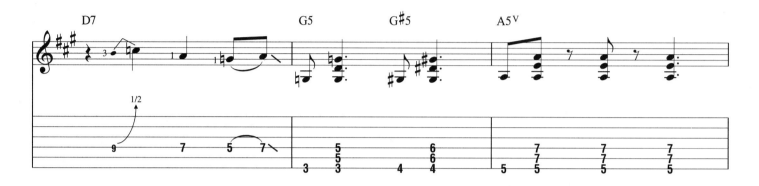

D7   G5 G#5 A5ᵛ

1. Well, the

Verse

A5

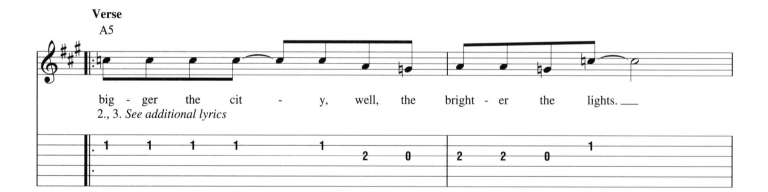

big - ger the cit - y, well, the bright - er the lights. ___
2., 3. *See additional lyrics*

Big - ger the dog, well, the hard - er the bite. ___   I don't know ___ where you

been last night, __ but I _____ think, ma - ma, you ain't _____ do - in' right. Say, I

Chorus

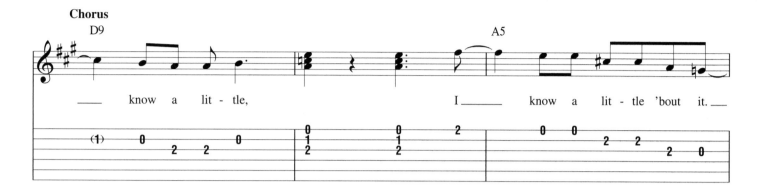

_____ know a lit - tle, I _____ know a lit - tle 'bout it. _____

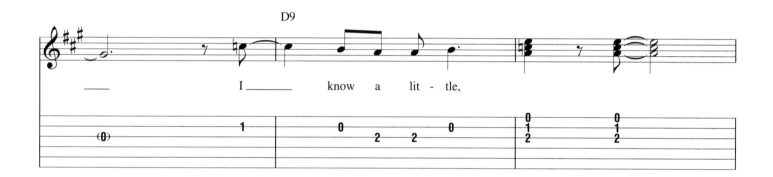

_____ I _____ know a lit - tle,

I know a lit - tle 'bout it. _____ I _____ know a lit - tle 'bout love. _____

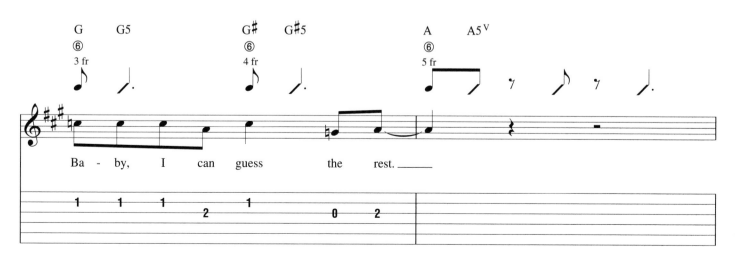

Ba - by, I can guess the rest. _____

Spoken: Baby, I want your best.

Additional Lyrics

2. Well, now, I don't read that daily news
   'Cause it ain't hard to figure where people get the blues.
   They can't dig what they can't use.
   If they stick to themselves, they'd be much less abused.

3. Well, now, you want me to be your only man.
   Said, listen up, mama, teach you all I can.
   Do right, baby, by your man.
   Don't worry, mama, teach you all I can.

Simple Man

Words and Music by Ronnie Van Zant and Gary Rossington

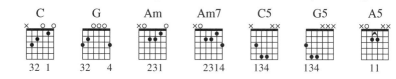

Tune down 1/2 step:
(low to high) E♭-A♭-D♭-G♭-B♭-E♭

Strum Pattern: 3
Pick Pattern: 3

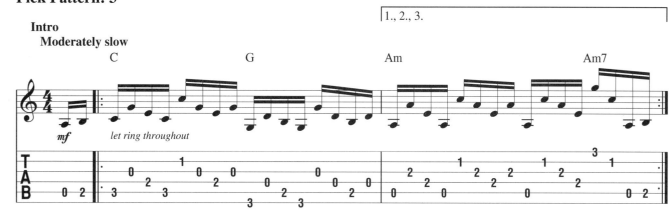

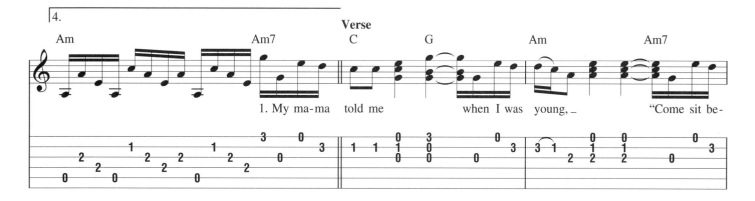

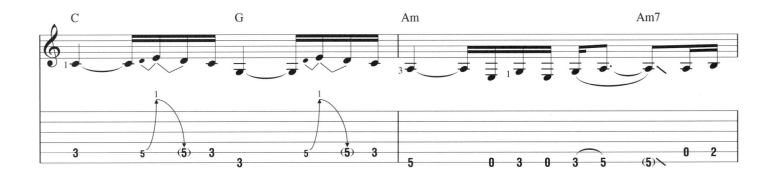

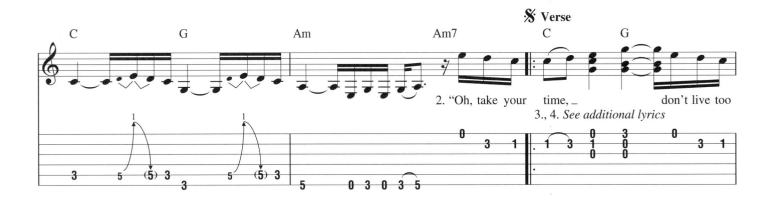

Verse

2. "Oh, take your time, __ don't live too fast. __ Trou-bles will come, __ and they will pass. __ Go find a

3., 4. *See additional lyrics*

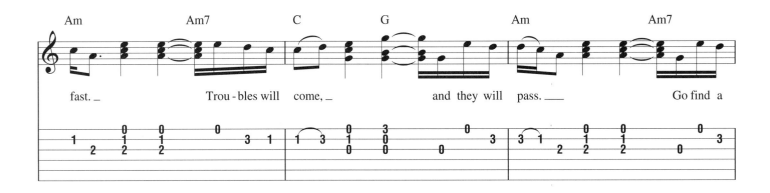

wom - an, yeah, and you'll find love. __ And don't for-get, son, there is some - one up __

Chorus

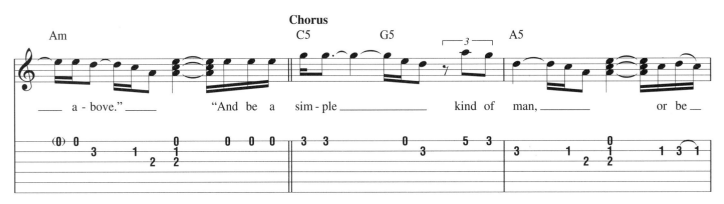

__ a - bove." __ "And be a sim - ple __ kind of man, __ or be __

Simple Man

Words and Music by Ronnie Van Zant and Gary Rossington

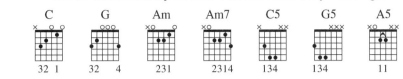

Tune down 1/2 step:
(low to high) E♭-A♭-D♭-G♭-B♭-E♭

Strum Pattern: 3
Pick Pattern: 3

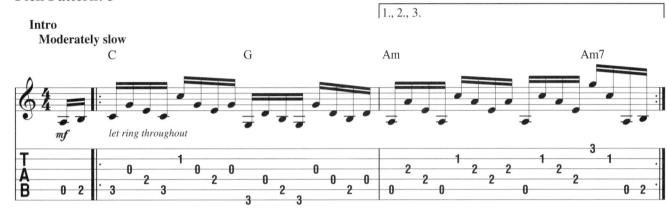

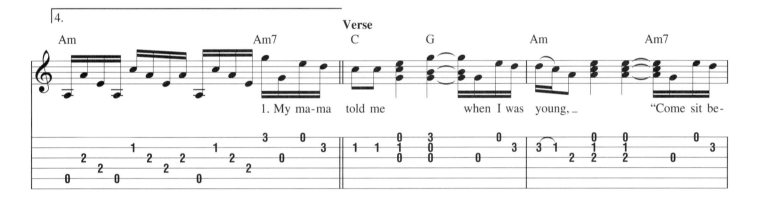

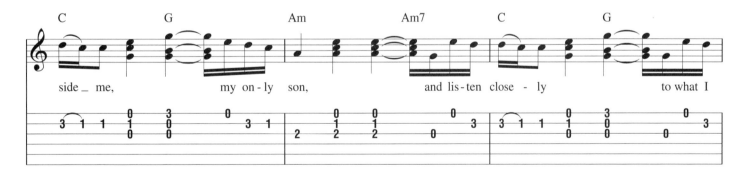

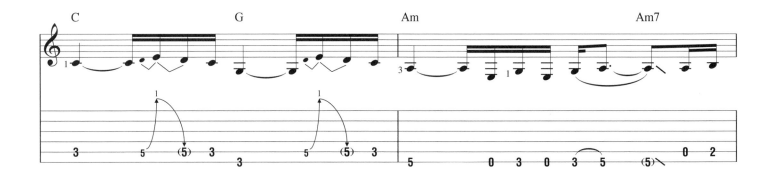

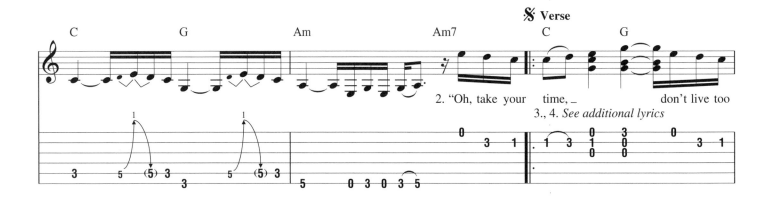

2. "Oh, take your   time, _   don't live too

3., 4. *See additional lyrics*

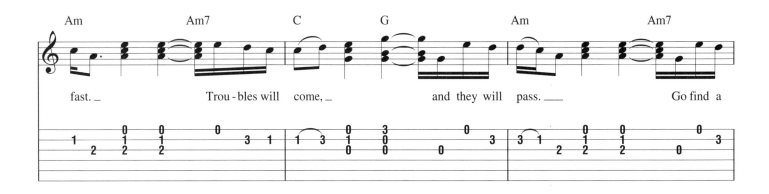

fast. _   Trou-bles will   come, _   and they will   pass. ___   Go find a

wom - an,   yeah,   and you'll find   love. _   And don't for-get, son,   there is some - one   up _

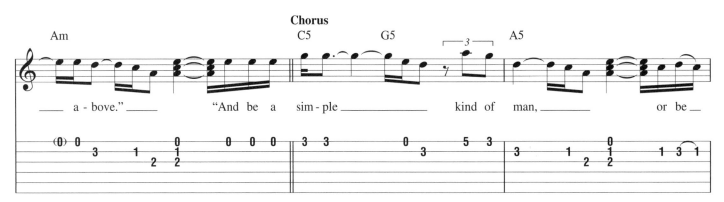

___ a - bove." ____   "And be a   sim - ple _____   kind of man, _____   or be _

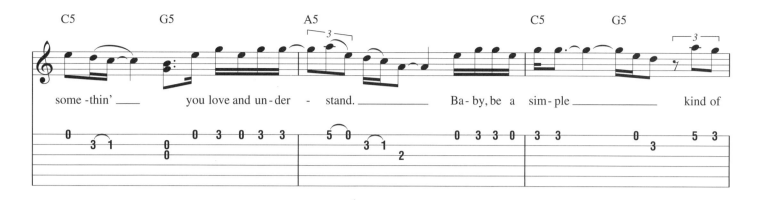

some -thin' ____ you love and un - der - stand. _____ Ba - by, be a sim - ple _____ kind of

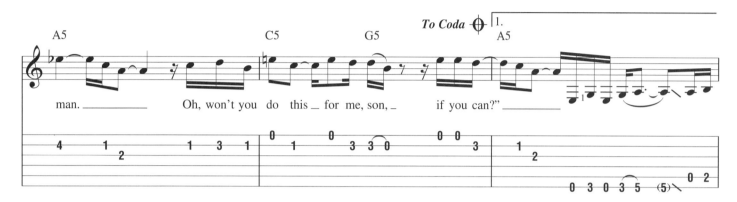

man. _____ Oh, won't you do this __ for me, son, __ if you can?" _____

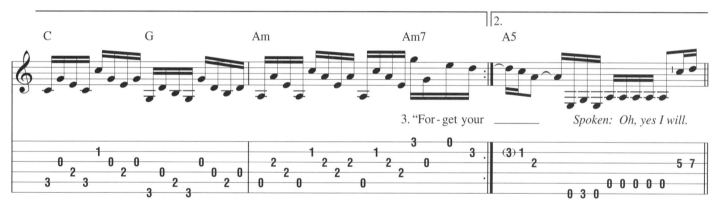

3. "For - get your _____ *Spoken: Oh, yes I will.*

Guitar Solo

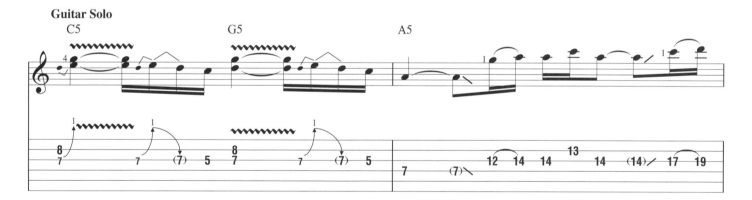

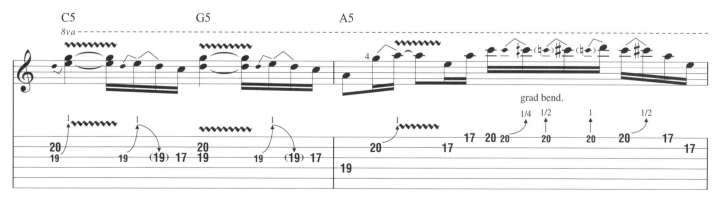

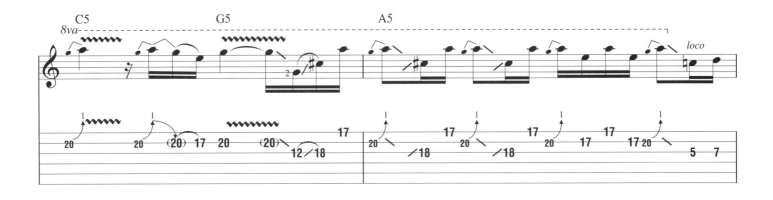

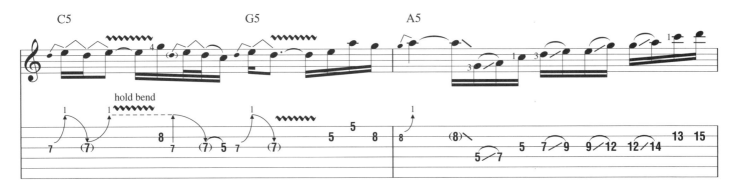

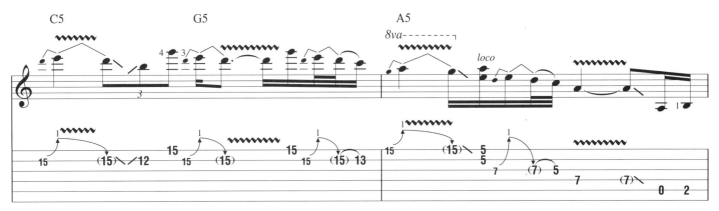

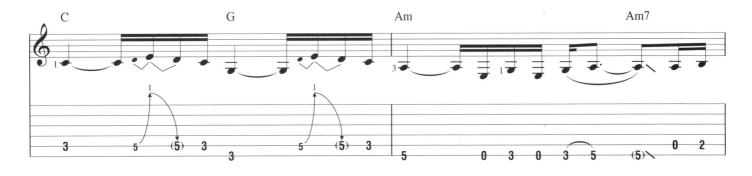

D.S. al Coda

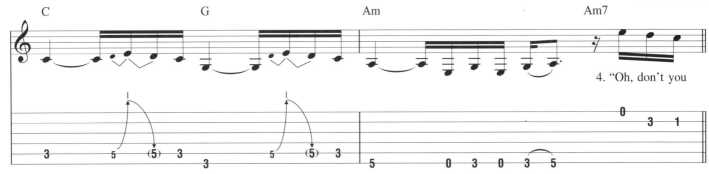

4. "Oh, don't you

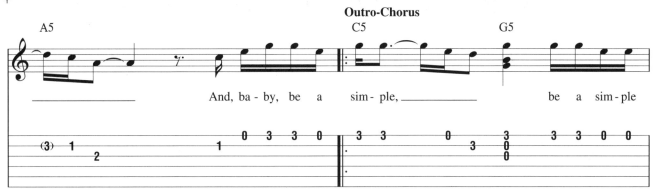

Coda

Outro-Chorus

And, ba - by, be a sim - ple, _____ be a sim - ple

Repeat and fade

man, _____ or be _ some - thin' _____ you love and un - der - stand. _____ Ba - by, be a

Additional Lyrics

3. "Forget your lust for the rich man's gold.
   All that you need is in your soul,
   And you can do this if you try.
   All that I want for you, my son,
   Is to be satisfied."

4. "Oh, don't you worry, you'll find yourself.
   Follow your heart, and nothin' else.
   And you can do this if you try.
   All that I want for you, my son,
   Is to be satisfied."

The Needle and the Spoon

Words and Music by Allen Collins and Ronnie Van Zant

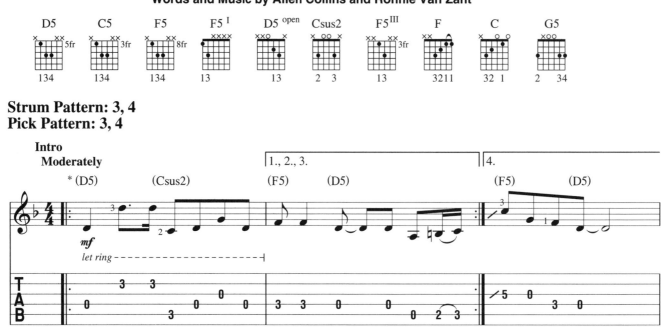

Strum Pattern: 3, 4
Pick Pattern: 3, 4

Intro
Moderately

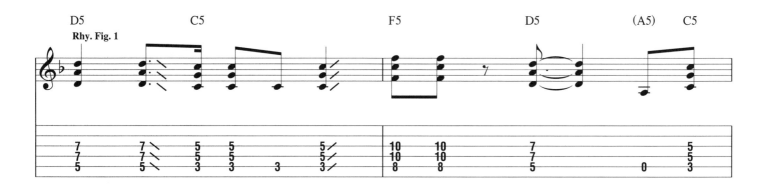

*Chord symbols in parentheses reflect implied harmony.

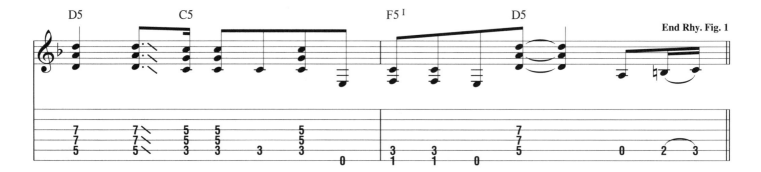

1. Thir-ty days, Lord, and thir-ty nights, _ I'm com-in' home _ on an
2., 3. *See additional lyrics*

Guitar Solo

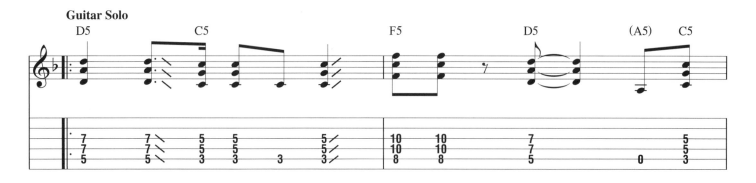

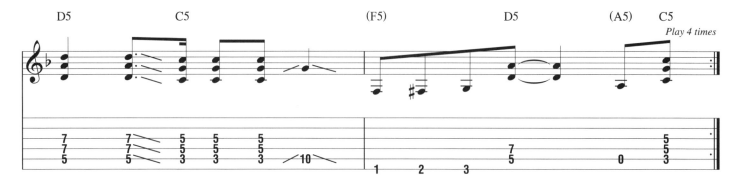

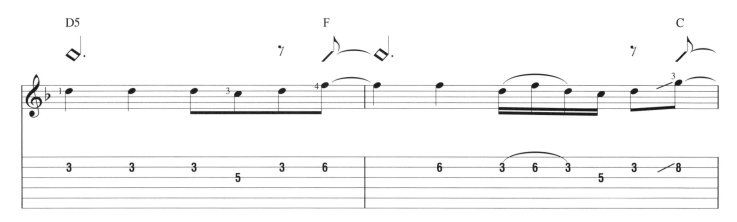

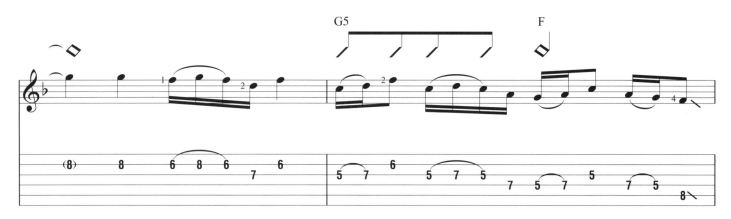

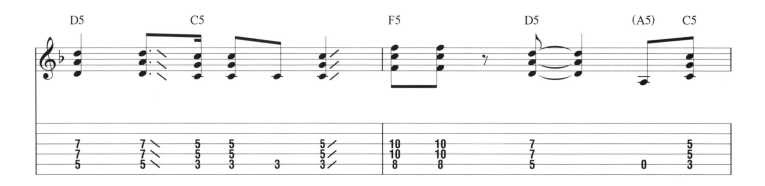

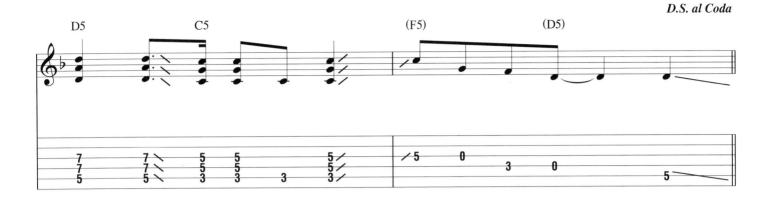

Coda

Outro

2nd time, voc. tacet

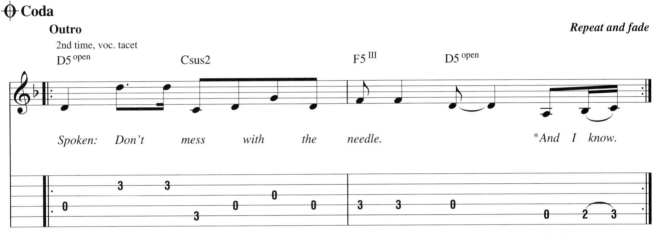

Spoken: Don't mess with the needle.   *And I know.

*w/ delay repeats

Additional Lyrics

2. I been feelin' so sick inside.
   Gonna hafta get better, Lord, before I die.
   Seven doctors couldn't help my head.
   They said, "You better quit, son, before you're dead."

Chorus 2. With the needle, with the spoon,
   With the trip to the moon.
   We gon' take you away.
   Lord, we gon' take you away.

3. I've seen a lot of people who thought they were cool,
   But then again, Lord, I've seen a lot of fools.
   Well, I hope you people, Lord, can hear what I say.
   You'll have your chance to hear this someday.

Chorus 3. Don't mess with the needle, or a spoon,
   Or in a trip to the moon.
   Gonna take you away.
   Lord, they're gonna carry you, boy.

Saturday Night Special

Words and Music by Edward King and Ronnie Van Zant

Strum Pattern: 1
Pick Pattern: 2

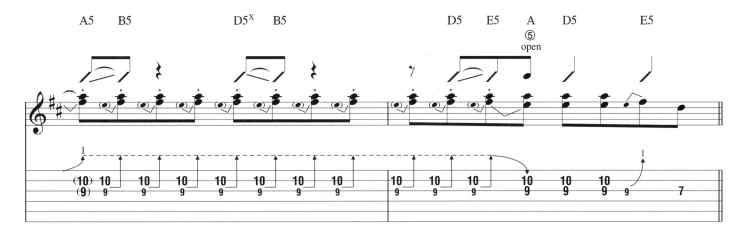

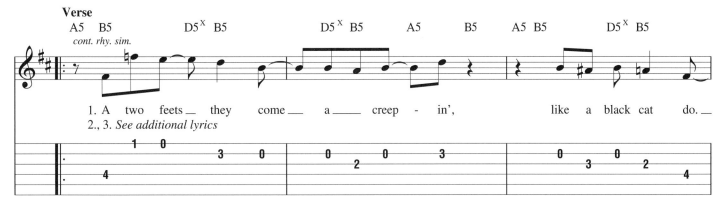

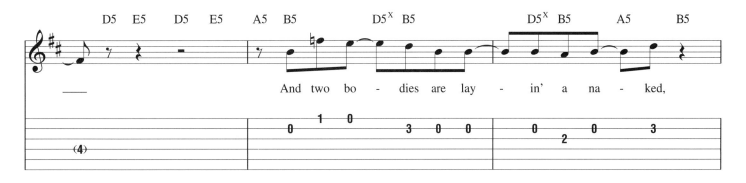

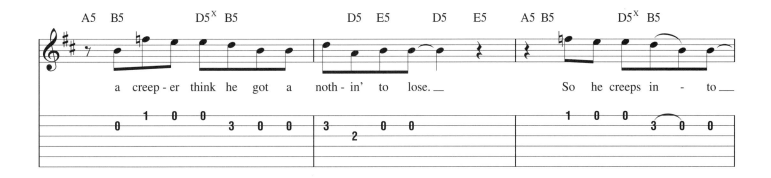

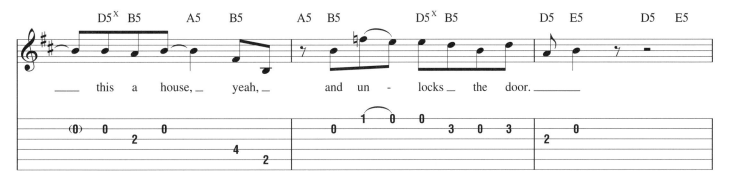

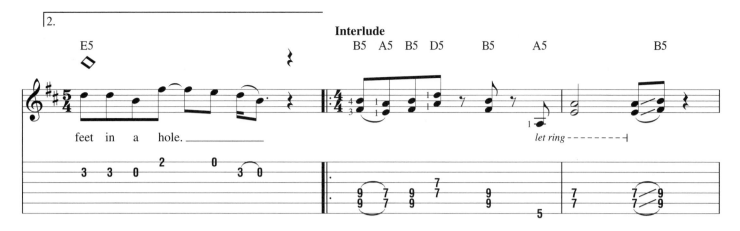

Interlude

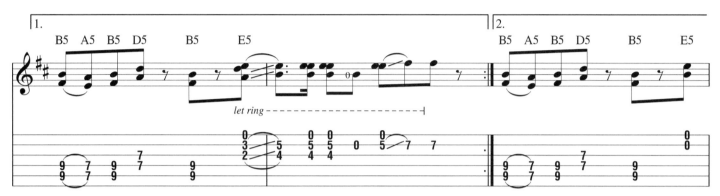

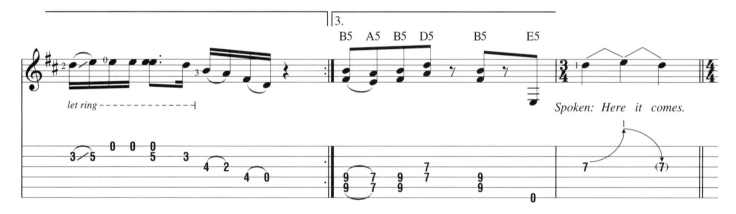

Guitar Solo

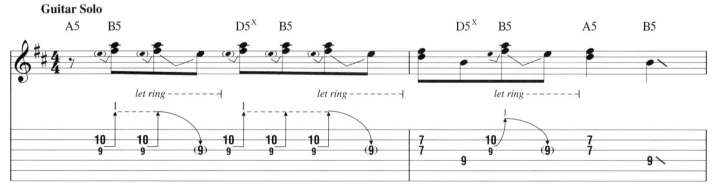

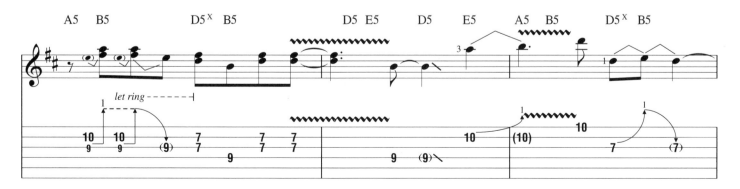

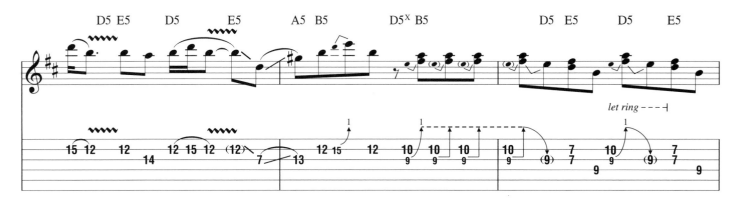

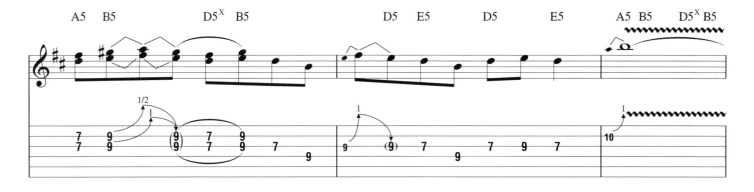

D.S. al Coda

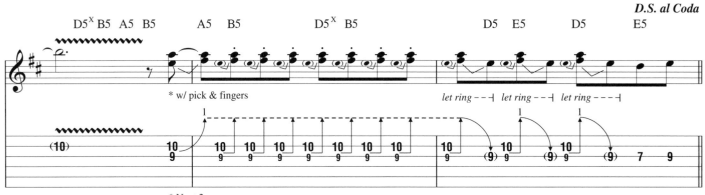

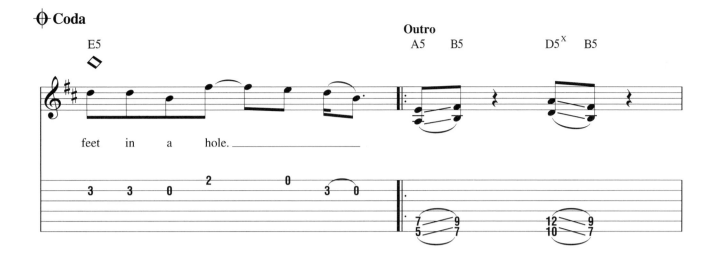

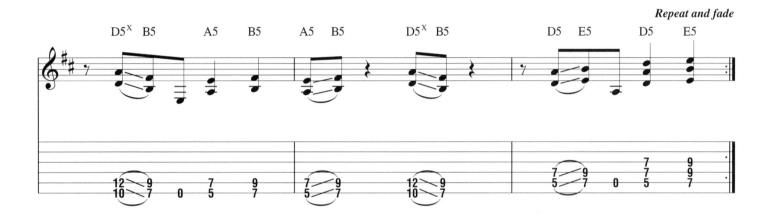

Additional Lyrics

2. Big Jim's been drinkin' a whiskey,
   And playin' poker on a losin' night.
   And pretty soon ol' Jim starts a thinkin',
   A somebody been cheatin' and lyin'.
   So Big Jim commenced to fightin',
   I wouldn't tell you no lies.
   Big Jim done a pulled his a pistol,
   Shot his friend a right between the eyes.

3. A handguns are made for killin',
   They ain't no good for nothin' else.
   And if you like to drink ol' whiskey,
   You might even shoot yourself.
   So why don't we dump 'em people,
   To the bottom of a sea?
   Before some ol' fool come around here
   Wanna shoot either you or me.

Sweet Home Alabama

Words and Music by Ronnie Van Zant, Ed King and Gary Rossington

Strum Pattern: 2
Pick Pattern: 4

Spoken: Turn it up.

1. Big ___ wheels ___ keep on turn-in', car-ry me home to see my

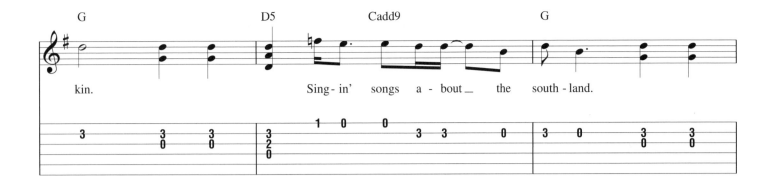

kin.   Sing - in' songs a - bout ___ the south - land.

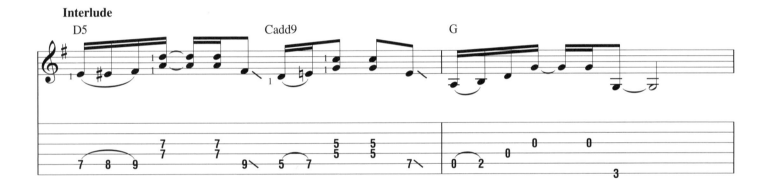

I miss Al - a - bam ___ y once a - gain, ___ and I think it's a sin. ___ *Spoken: Yes.*

Interlude

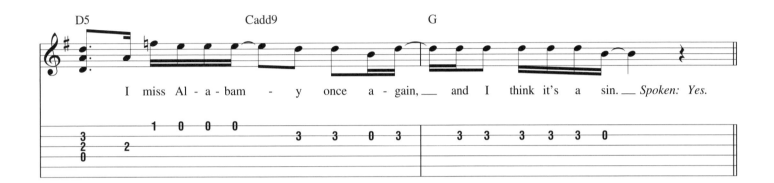

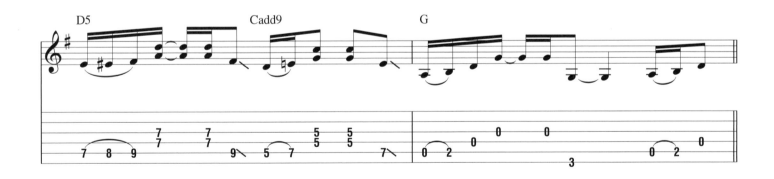

%̸ Verse

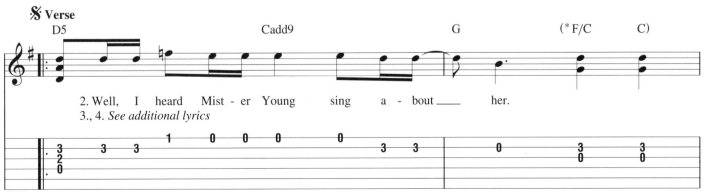

2. Well, I heard Mist - er Young   sing   a - bout ___   her.
3., 4. *See additional lyrics*

* Play on 3rd Verse only

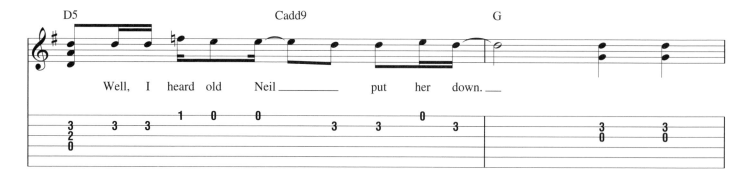

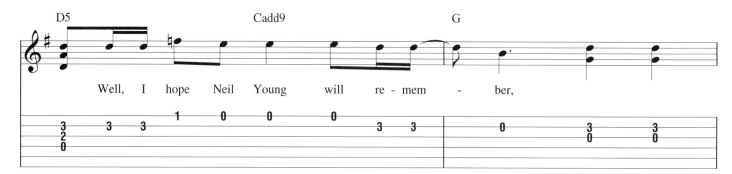

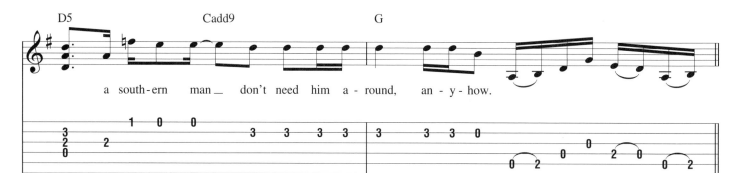

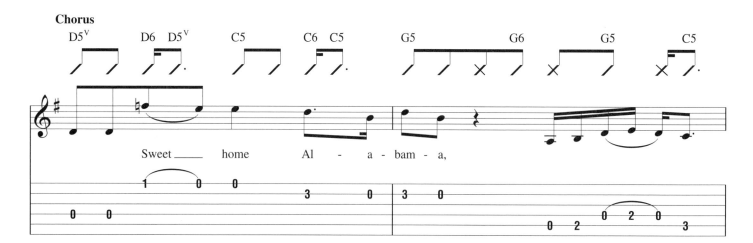

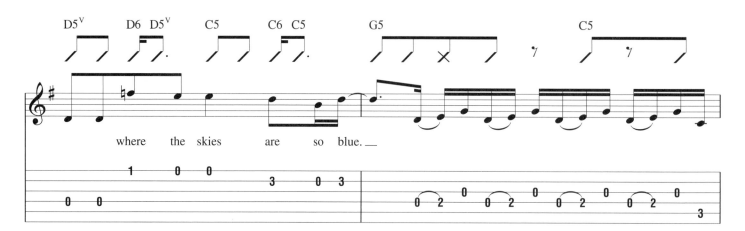

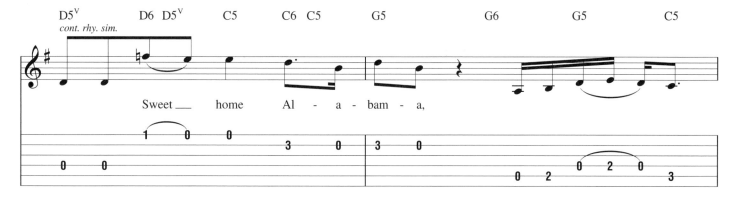

Sweet ___ home Al - a - bam - a,

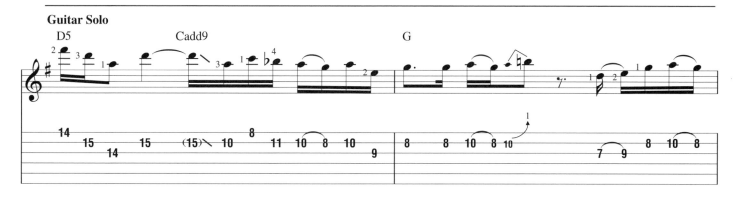

To Coda ⊕

1.

Lord, I'm com - in' home to you.

Guitar Solo

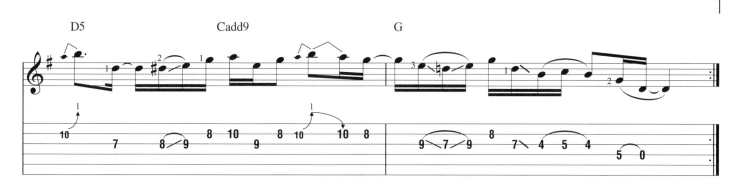

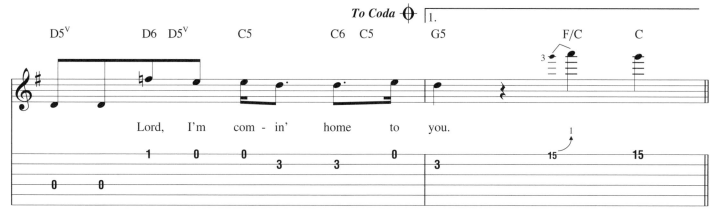

2.

Guitar Solo

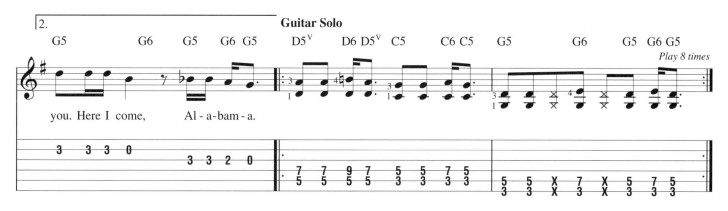

you. Here I come, Al - a-bam - a.

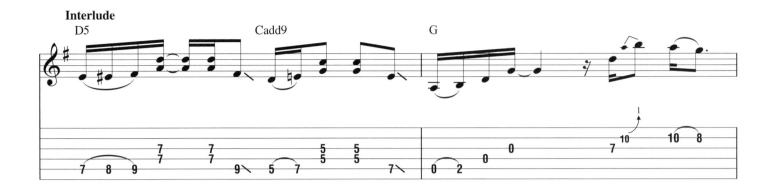

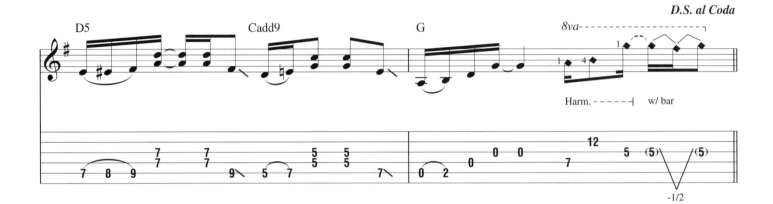

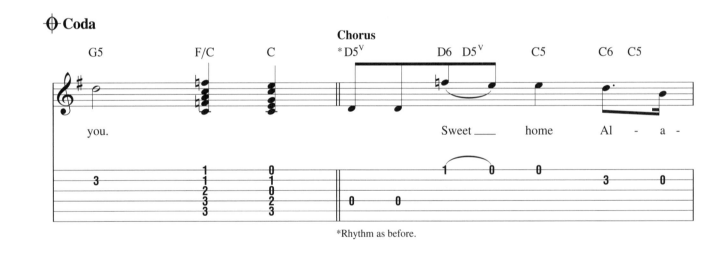

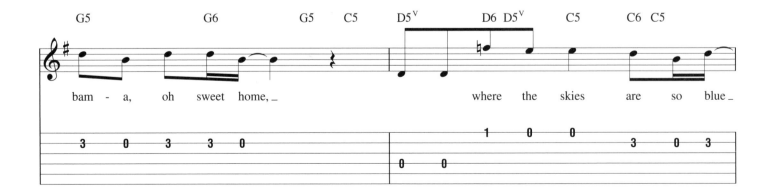

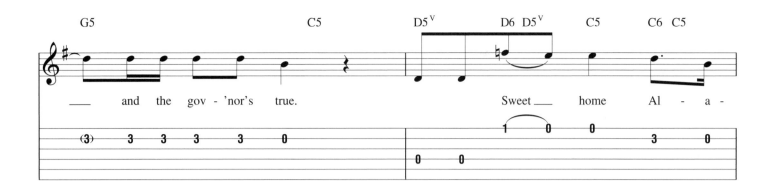

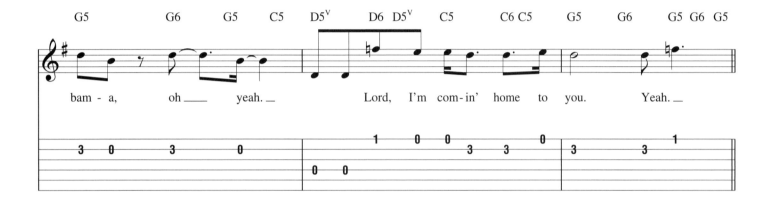

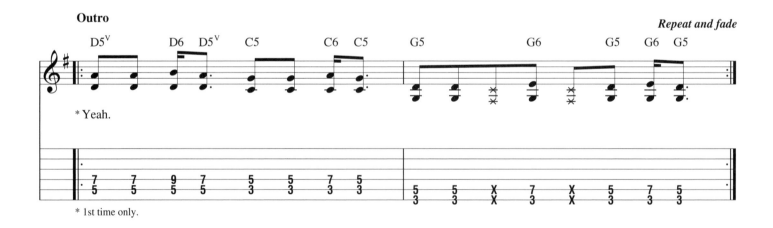

Additional Lyrics

3. In Birmingham they love the gov'nor. Boo, boo, boo.
   Now we all did what we could do.
   Now Watergate does not bother me,
   Does your conscience bother you? Tell the truth.

4. Now Muscle Shoals has got the Swampers,
   An' they been known to pick a song or two. (Yes they do!)
   Lord, they get me off so much,
   They pick me up when I'm feelin' blue 'n' now how 'bout you?

That Smell

Words and Music by Ronnie Van Zant and Allen Collins

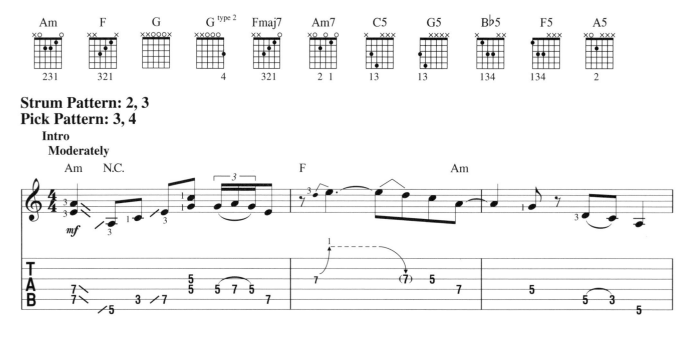

Strum Pattern: 2, 3
Pick Pattern: 3, 4

Intro
Moderately

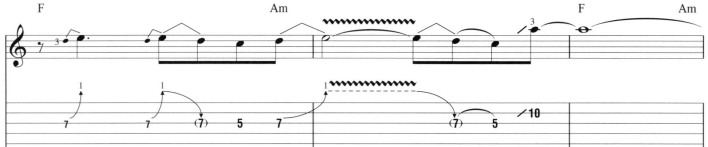

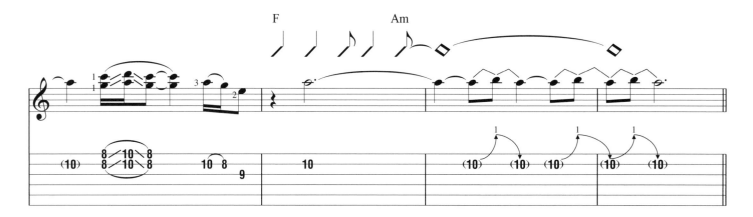

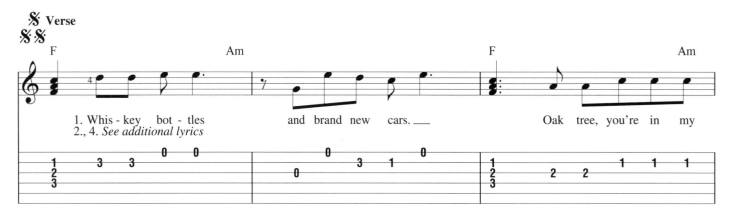

1. Whis-key bot-tles and brand new cars. ___ Oak tree, you're in my
2., 4. *See additional lyrics*

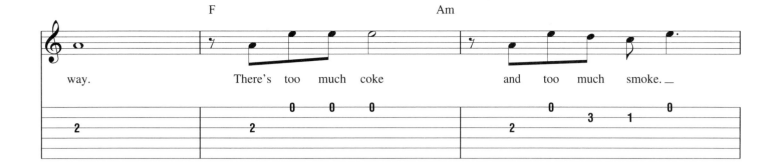

way.   There's too much coke   and too much smoke. __

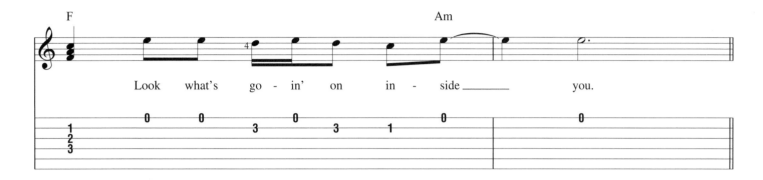

Look   what's   go - in'   on   in - side _____   you.

Chorus

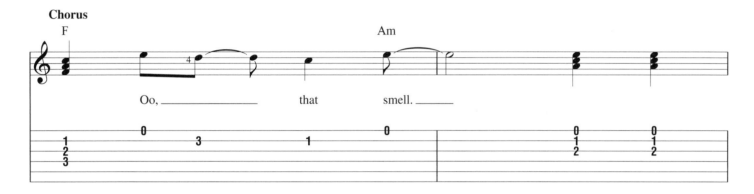

Oo, _____   that   smell. _____

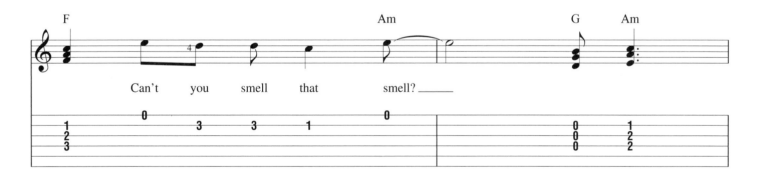

Can't   you   smell   that   smell? _____

To Coda **1** ⊕
To Coda **2** ⊕

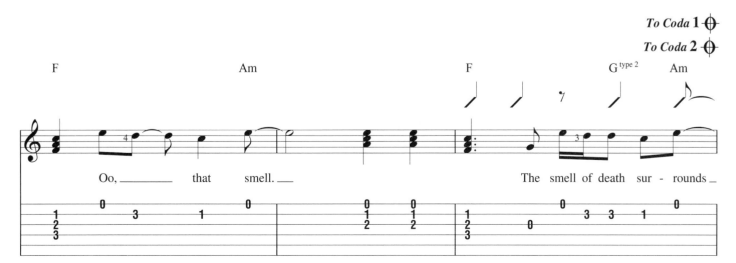

Oo, _____   that   smell. __   The   smell   of   death   sur - rounds __

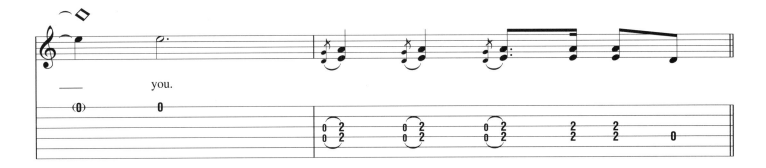

Interlude

2nd time, D.S. al Coda 1

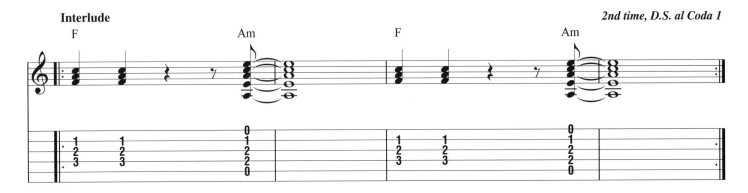

Coda 1

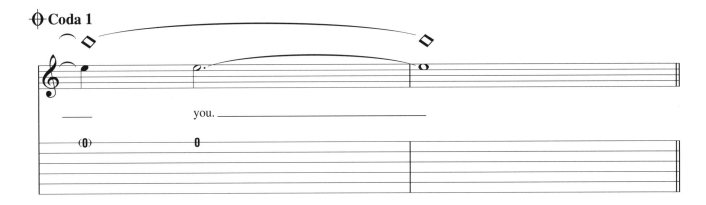

you.

Verse

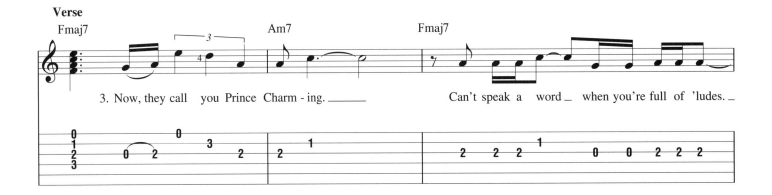

3. Now, they call you Prince Charm - ing. _____ Can't speak a word _ when you're full of 'ludes. _

Say you'll be al - right come to - mor - row, but to -

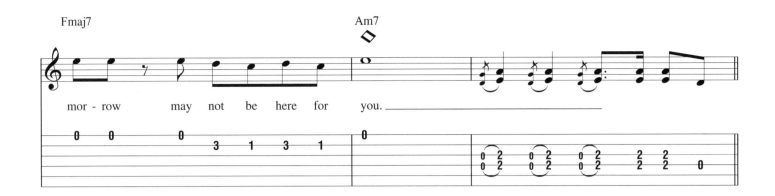

mor - row   may   not   be   here   for   you.

Chorus

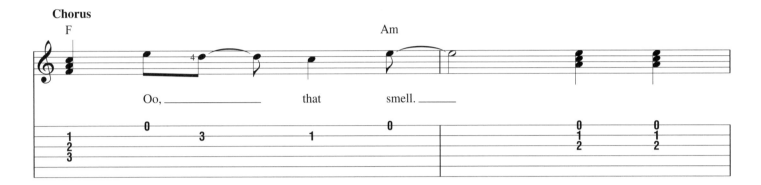

Oo, _____ that   smell. _____

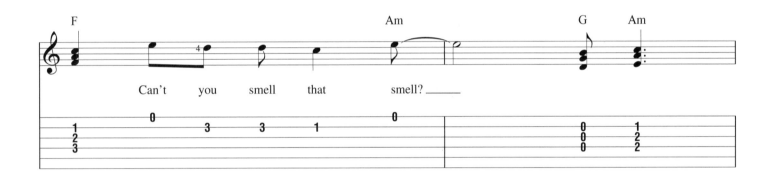

Can't   you   smell   that   smell? _____

Oo, _____ that   smell. ___   The   smell   of   death   sur - rounds _

Interlude

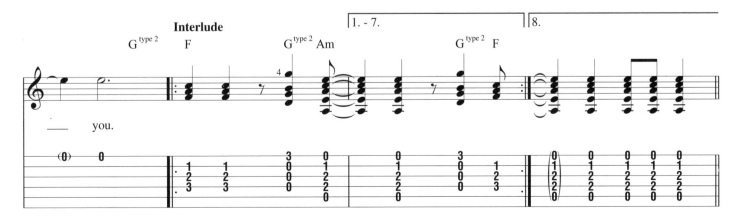

_____   you.

Bridge

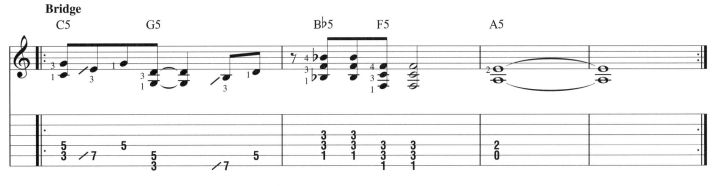

2nd time, D.S.S. al Coda 2

Interlude

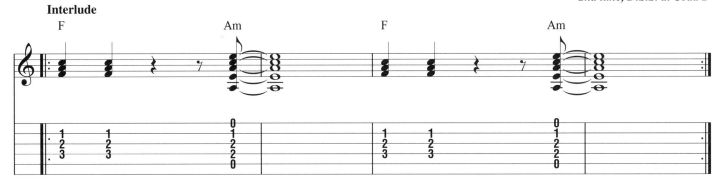

⊕ **Coda 2**

Chorus

___ you.   Oo, _____ that smell. ___

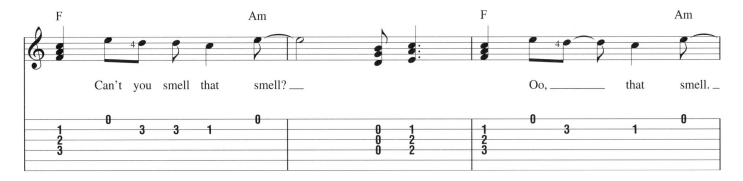

Can't you smell that   smell? ___   Oo, _____ that smell. ___

___   The smell of death sur - rounds ___ you.

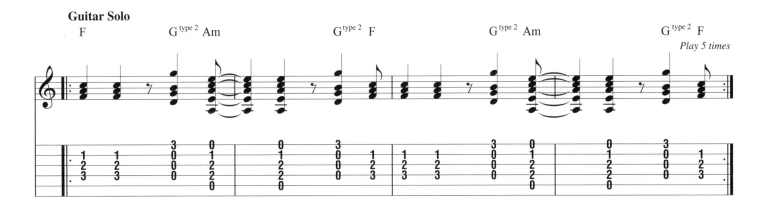

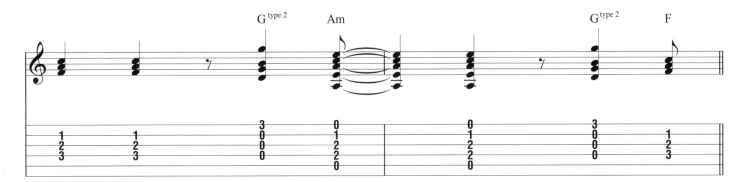

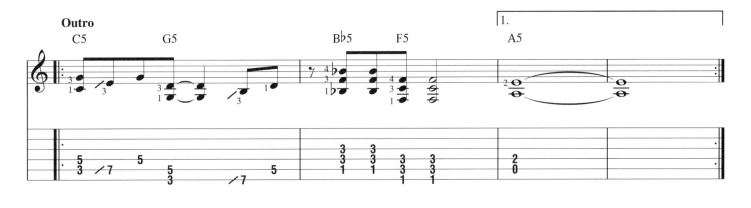

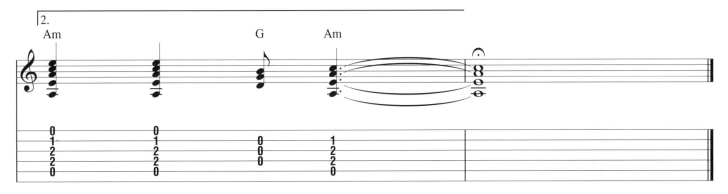

Additional Lyrics

2. Angel of darkness is upon you,
    Stuck a needle in your arm. *(You fool, you.)*
    So take another toke, have a blow for your nose.
    One more drink, fool, will drown you, ah. *(Hell, yeah.)*

4. One little problem that confronts you,
    Got a monkey on your back.
    Just one more fix, Lord, might do the trick.
    One hell of a price for you to get your kicks. *(Hell, yeah.)*

Tuesday's Gone

Words and Music by Allen Collins and Ronnie Van Zant

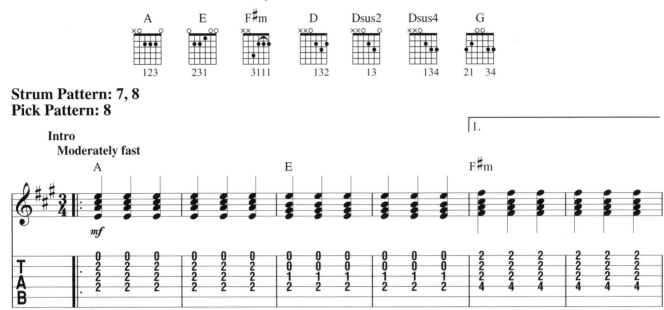

Strum Pattern: 7, 8
Pick Pattern: 8

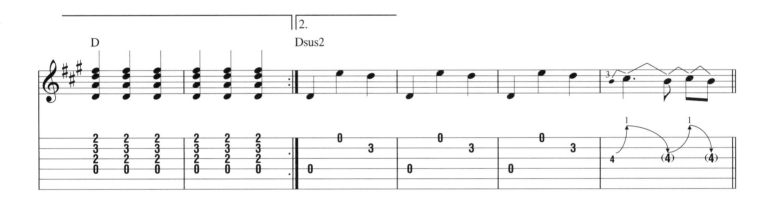

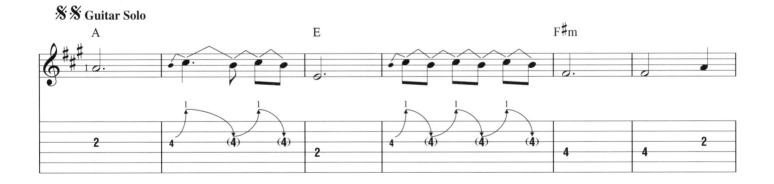

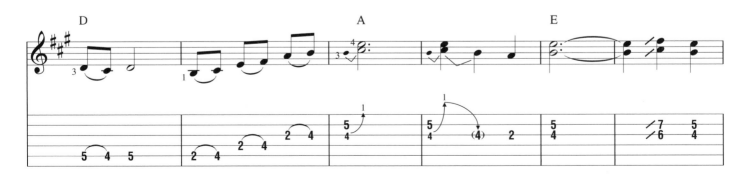

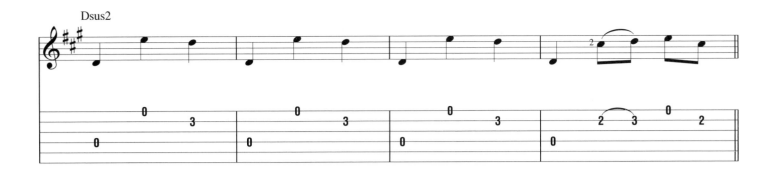

Verse

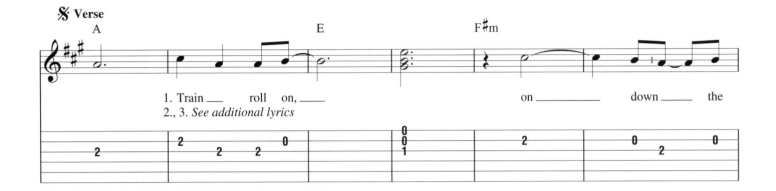

1. Train roll on, on down the
2., 3. *See additional lyrics*

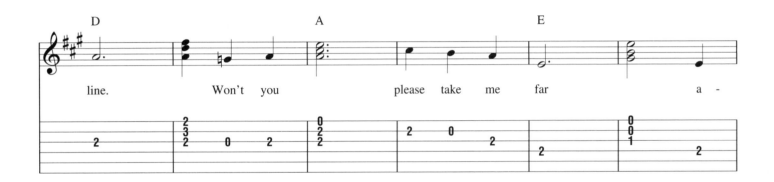

line. Won't you please take me far a -

way? Now, I feel the wind

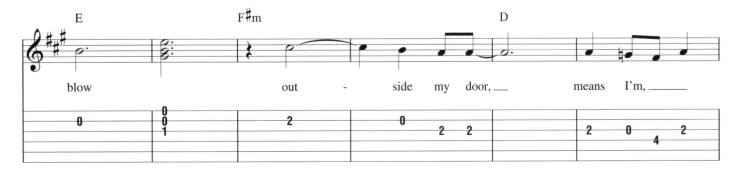

blow out - side my door, means I'm,

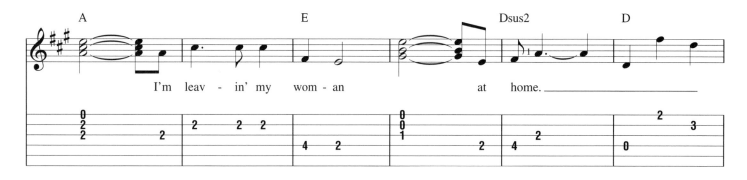

I'm leav - in' my wom - an at home.

Chorus

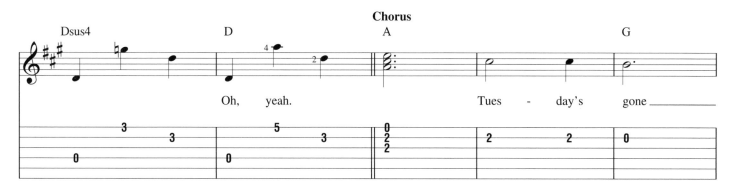

Oh, yeah. Tues - day's gone

To Coda **1** 𝄌

To Coda **2** 𝄌

— with the wind.

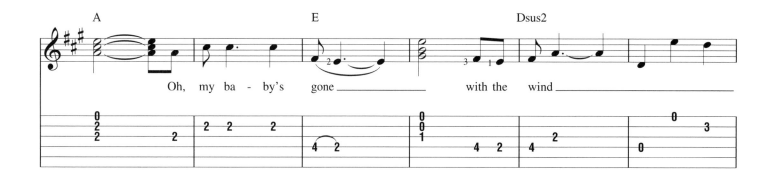

Oh, my ba - by's gone with the wind

Guitar Solo

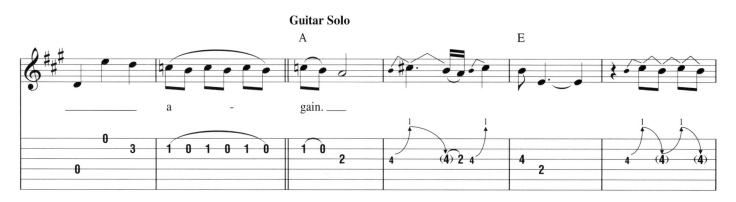

— a - gain.

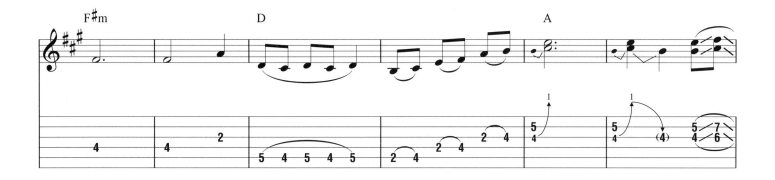

D.S. al Coda 1

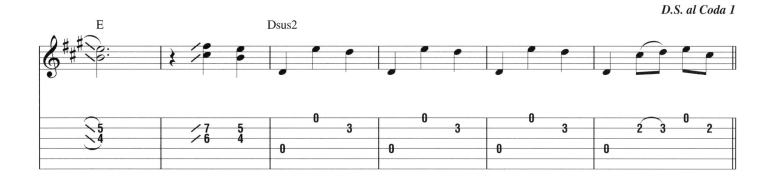

Coda 1

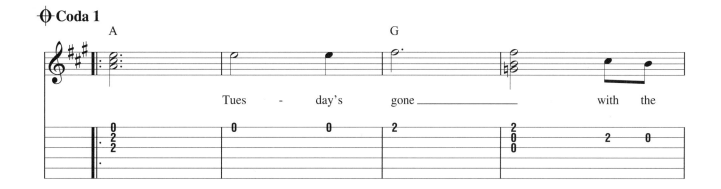

Tues - day's gone _____ with the

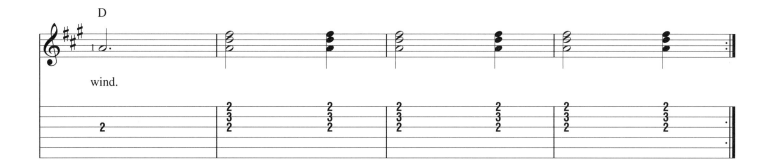

wind.

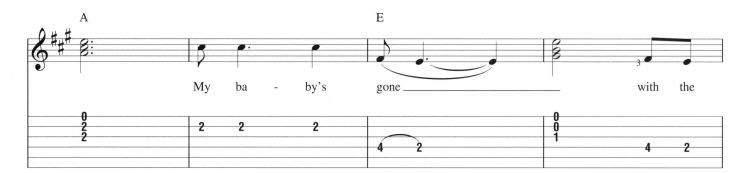

My ba - by's gone _____ with the

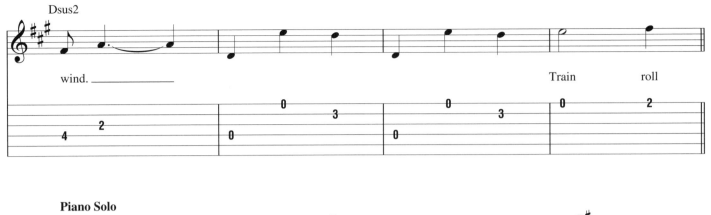

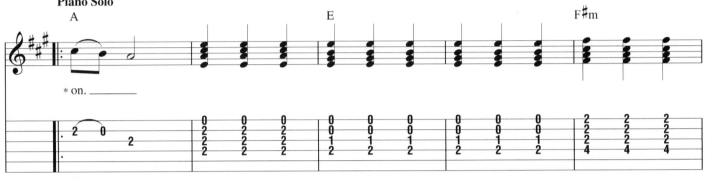

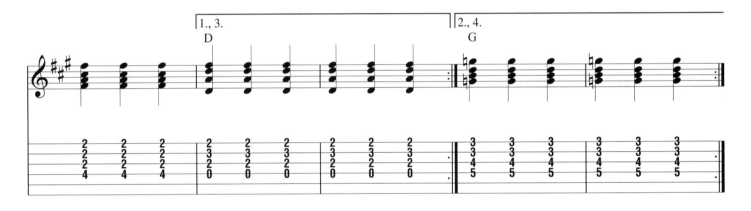

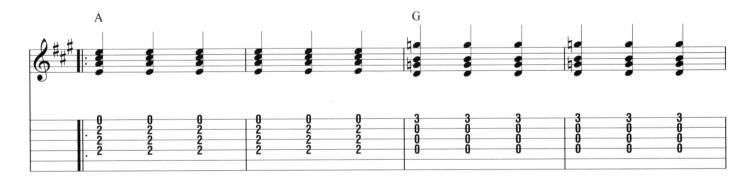

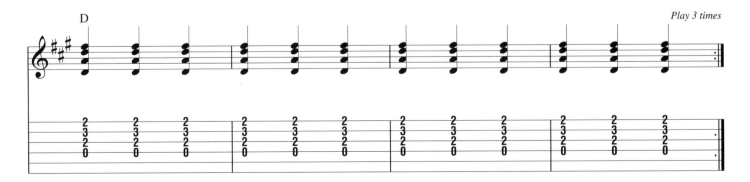

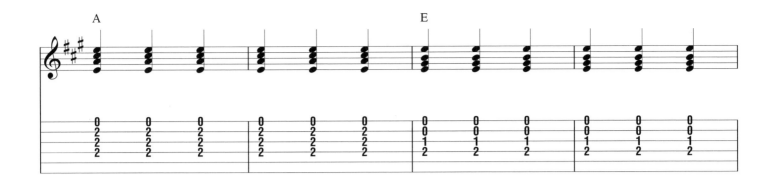

D.S.S. al Coda 2

⊕ **Coda 2**

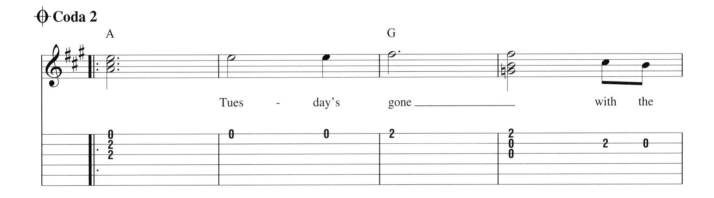

Tues - day's gone _____ with the

wind.

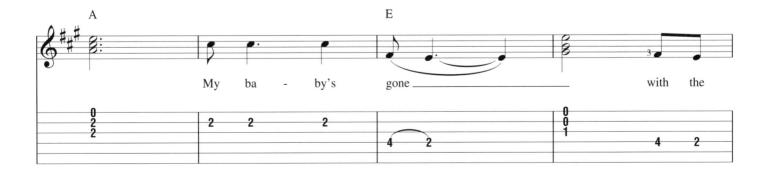

My ba - by's gone _____ with the

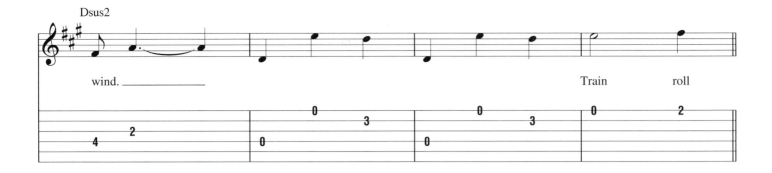

Dsus2

wind. _____   Train   roll

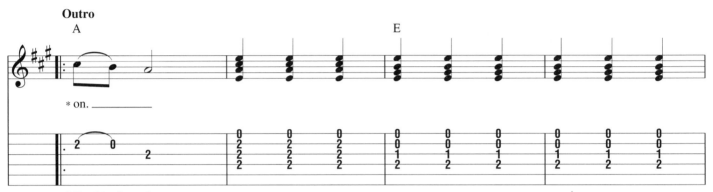

Outro

A   E

* on. _____

* Vocal 1st time only.
  Strum A chord on repeats.

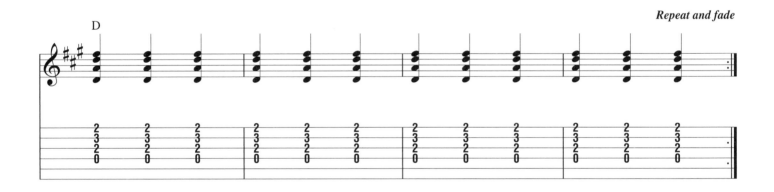

Repeat and fade

D

Additional Lyrics

2. And I don't know, oh, where I'm goin'.
   I just want to be left alone.
   Well, when this train ends, I'll try again.
   I'm leavin' my woman at home, oh yeah.

3. Train roll on a many miles from home,
   See I'm, I'm ridin' my blues away, yeah.
   But Tuesday, you see, a she had to be free, Lord.
   Somehow I got to carry on, oh yeah.

What's Your Name

Words and Music by Gary Rossington and Ronnie Van Zant

Strum Pattern: 1
Pick Pattern: 2

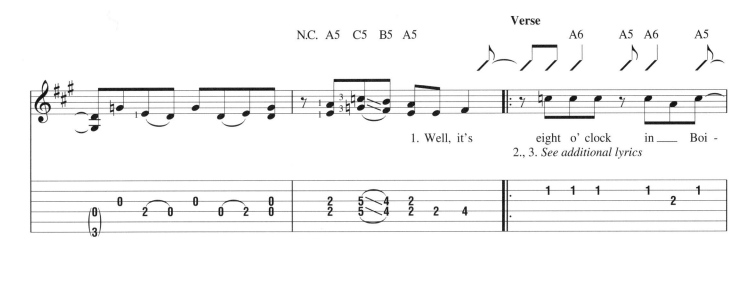

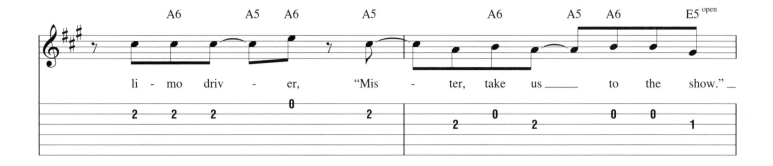

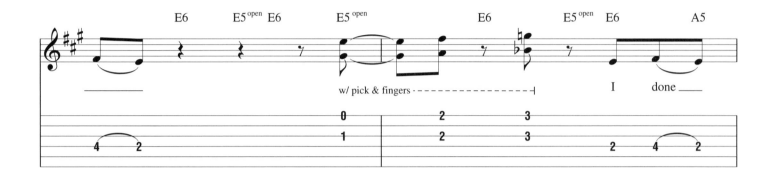

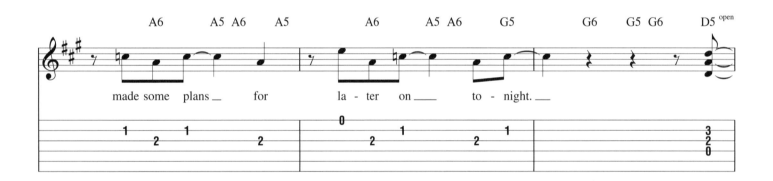

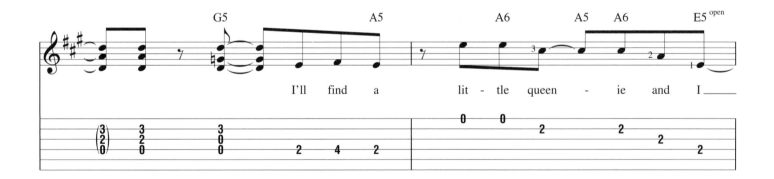

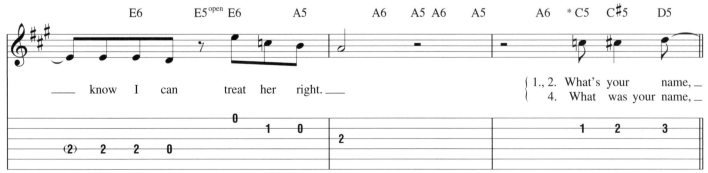

* Intro rhythm, simile

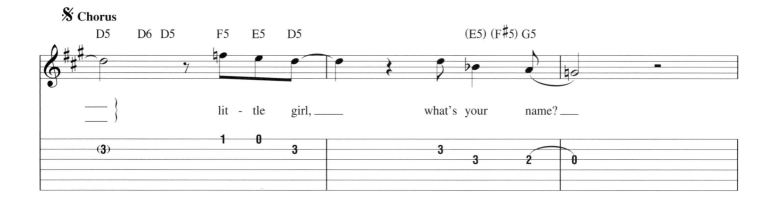

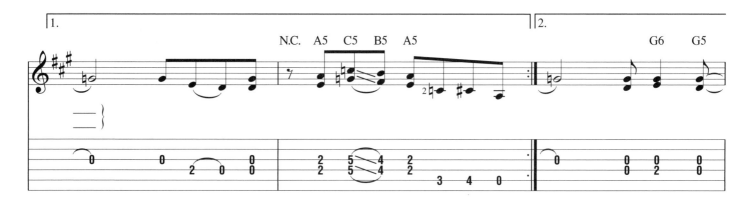

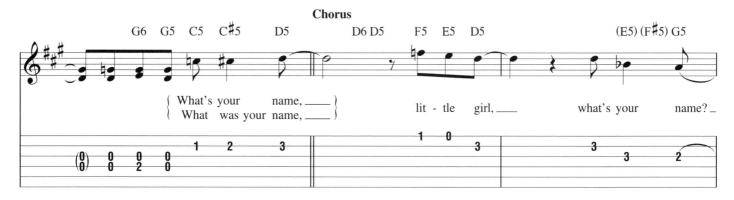

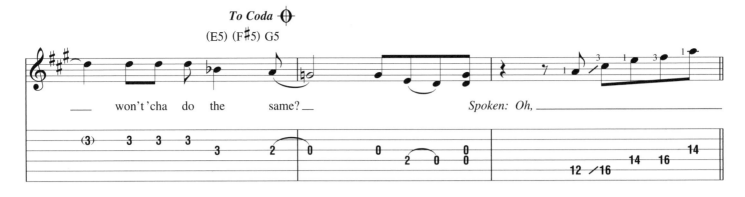

To Coda ⊕

(E5) (F♯5) G5

___ won't'cha do the same? ___   _Spoken: Oh,_ ___

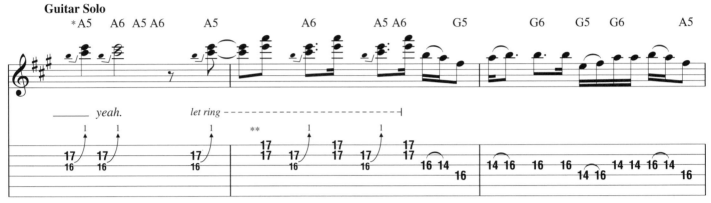

Guitar Solo

*A5 A6 A5 A6   A5   A6   A5 A6   G5   G6   G5 G6   A5

___ yeah.   _let ring_ - - - - - - - - - - - - - - - - -

* Verse rhythm, simile   ** barre pinky

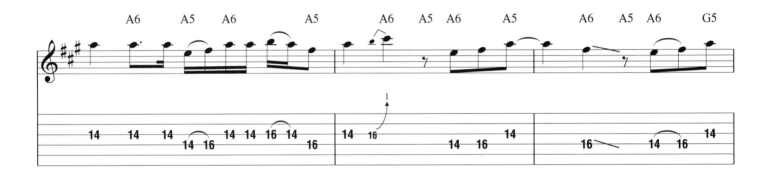

A6   A5 A6   A5   A6   A5 A6   A5   A6   A5 A6   G5

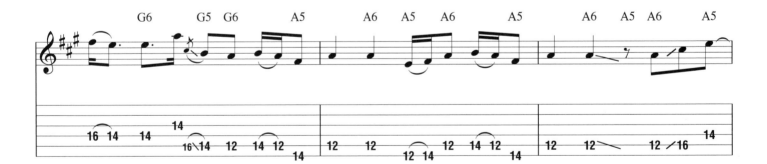

G6   G5 G6   A5   A6   A5   A6   A5   A6   A5 A6   A5

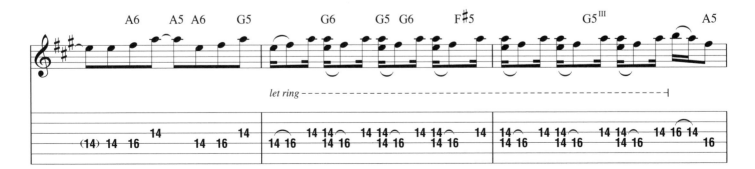

A6   A5 A6   G5   G6   G5 G6   F♯5   G5ᴵᴵᴵ   A5

let ring -

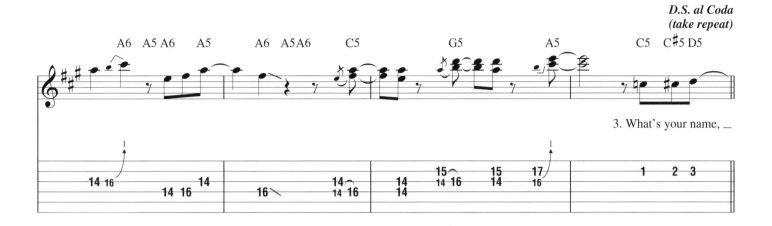

3. What's your name, __

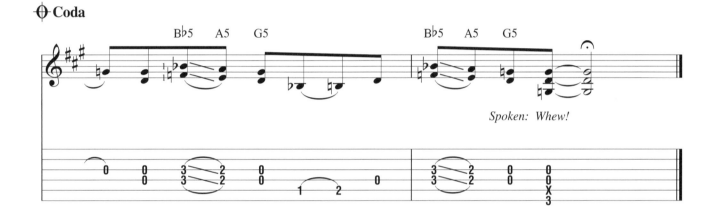

Spoken: Whew!

Additional Lyrics

2. Back at the hotel, Lord, we got such a mess.
   It seems that one of the crew had a go with one of the guests. Ah, yes.
   Well, the police said we can't drink in the bar. What a shame.
   Won't you come upstairs, girl, and have a drink of champagne?

3. Nine o'clock the next day, I'm ready to go.
   I got six hundred miles to ride to do one more show, oh, no.
   Can I get you a taxi home? It sure was grand.
   When I come back next year I wanna see you again.

You Got That Right

Words and Music by Steve Earl Gaines and Ronnie Van Zant

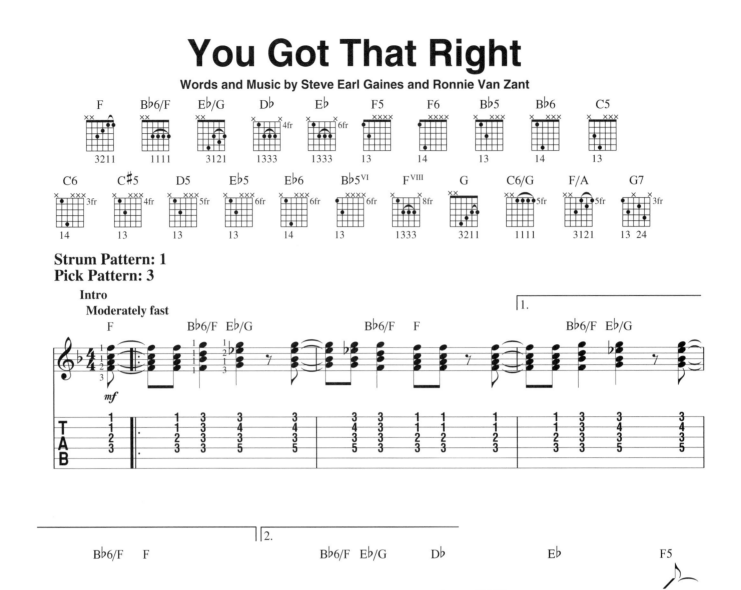

Strum Pattern: 1
Pick Pattern: 3

*Vth position, next 7 meas.

1. Well, I've heard

lots of peo-ple say they're gon-na set-tle down. You don't see their fac - es and they

2., 4. *See additional lyrics*
3. *Instrumental*

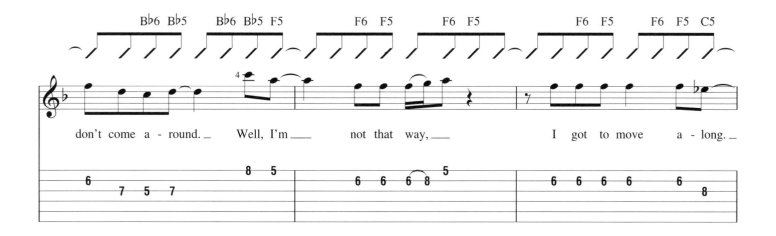

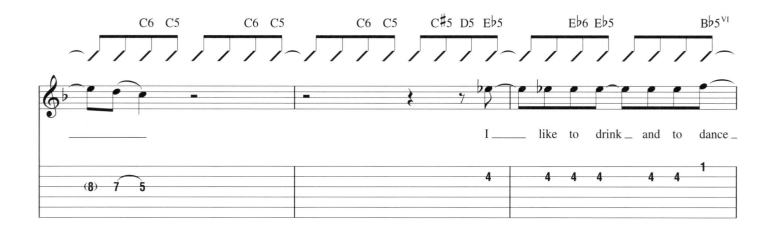

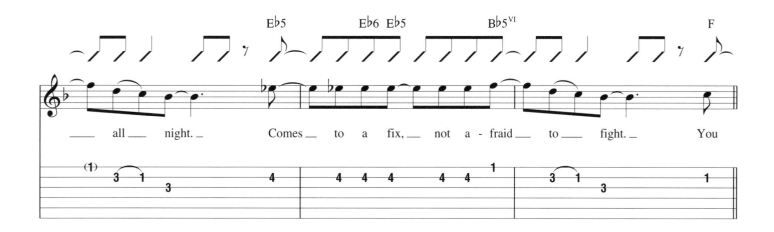

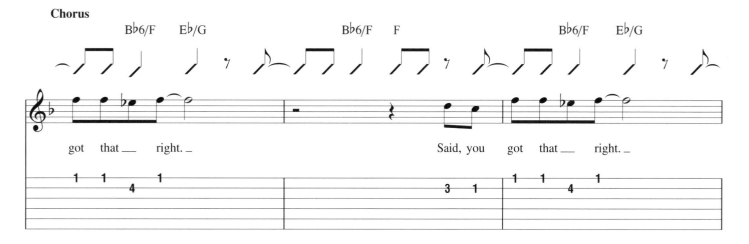

Sure ____ got that right.

2. Seems ____
4. Trav -

Well, you got that ____ right. ____

Sure ____

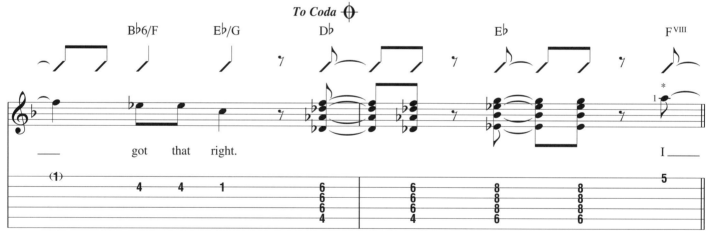

To Coda ⊕

____ got that right.

I ____

Vth position, next 5 meas.

Bridge

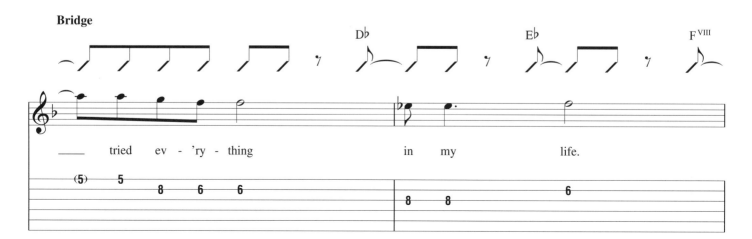

____ tried ev - 'ry - thing in my life.

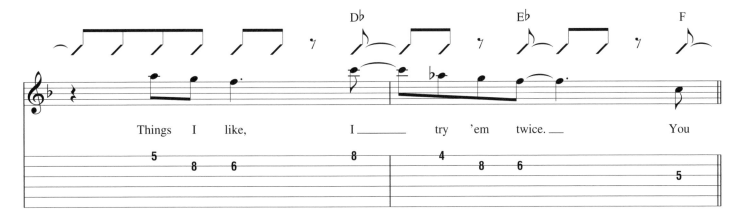

Things I like, I _____ try 'em twice. _____ You

Chorus

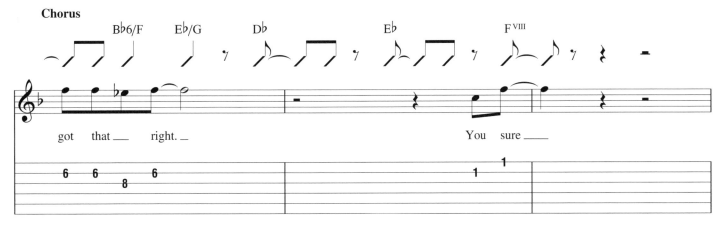

got that _____ right. _____ You sure _____

D.S. al Coda
(take repeat)

got that right.

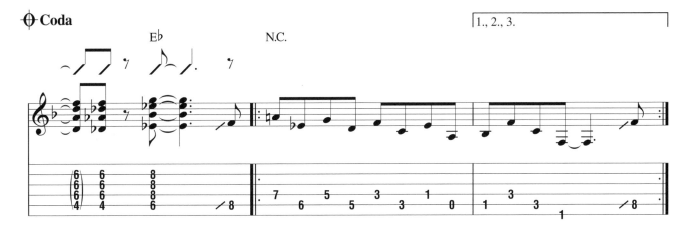

1., 2., 3.

Uh!

Guitar Solo

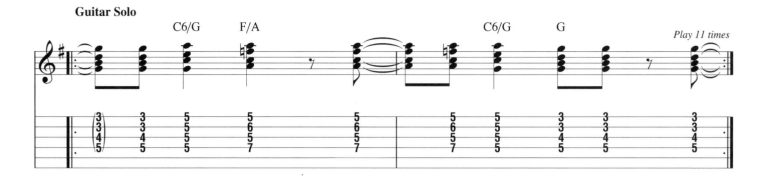

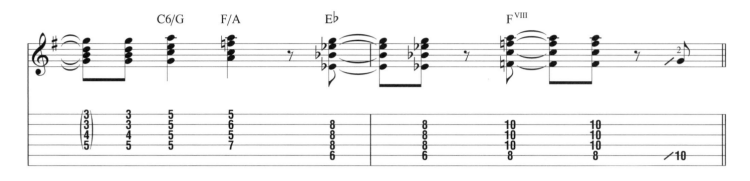

Outro

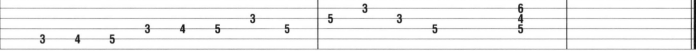

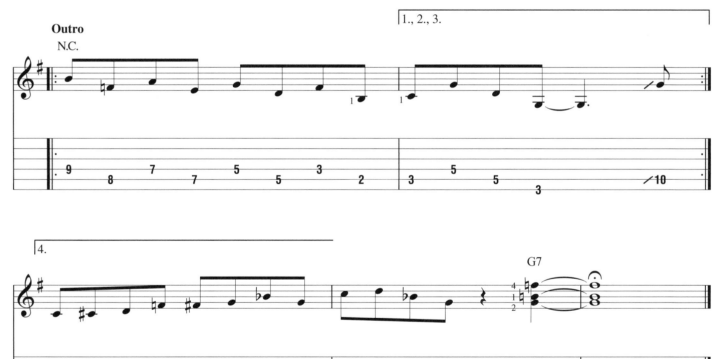

Additional Lyrics

2. Seems so long I been out on my own.
   Travel light and I'm always alone.
   Guess I was born with a travelin' bone.
   When my time's up, I'll hold my own.
   You won't find me in an old folks home.

3. Trav'lin' 'round the world just singing my song.
   I got to go, Lord, I can't stay long.
   Here comes that old travelin' jones once again.
   I like to drink and to dance all night.
   Comes to a fix, not afraid to fight.

EASY GUITAR
WITH NOTES & TAB

This series features simplified arrangements with notes, tab, chord charts, and strum and pick patterns.

MIXED FOLIOS

00702287	Acoustic	$19.99
00702002	Acoustic Rock Hits for Easy Guitar	$15.99
00702166	All-Time Best Guitar Collection	$19.99
00702232	Best Acoustic Songs for Easy Guitar	$16.99
00119835	Best Children's Songs	$16.99
00703055	The Big Book of Nursery Rhymes & Children's Songs	$16.99
00698978	Big Christmas Collection	$19.99
00702394	Bluegrass Songs for Easy Guitar	$15.99
00289632	Bohemian Rhapsody	$19.99
00703387	Celtic Classics	$16.99
00224808	Chart Hits of 2016-2017	$14.99
00267383	Chart Hits of 2017-2018	$14.99
00334293	Chart Hits of 2019-2020	$16.99
00403479	Chart Hits of 2021-2022	$16.99
00702149	Children's Christian Songbook	$9.99
00702028	Christmas Classics	$8.99
00101779	Christmas Guitar	$14.99
00702141	Classic Rock	$8.95
00159642	Classical Melodies	$12.99
00253933	Disney/Pixar's Coco	$16.99
00702203	CMT's 100 Greatest Country Songs	$34.99
00702283	The Contemporary Christian Collection	$16.99

00196954	Contemporary Disney	$19.99
00702239	Country Classics for Easy Guitar	$24.99
00702257	Easy Acoustic Guitar Songs	$17.99
00702041	Favorite Hymns for Easy Guitar	$12.99
00222701	Folk Pop Songs	$17.99
00126894	Frozen	$14.99
00333922	Frozen 2	$14.99
00702286	Glee	$16.99
00702160	The Great American Country Songbook	$19.99
00702148	Great American Gospel for Guitar	$14.99
00702050	Great Classical Themes for Easy Guitar	$9.99
00275088	The Greatest Showman	$17.99
00148030	Halloween Guitar Songs	$14.99
00702273	Irish Songs	$14.99
00192503	Jazz Classics for Easy Guitar	$16.99
00702275	Jazz Favorites for Easy Guitar	$17.99
00702274	Jazz Standards for Easy Guitar	$19.99
00702162	Jumbo Easy Guitar Songbook	$24.99
00232285	La La Land	$16.99
00702258	Legends of Rock	$14.99
00702189	MTV's 100 Greatest Pop Songs	$34.99
00702272	1950s Rock	$16.99
00702271	1960s Rock	$16.99
00702270	1970s Rock	$24.99
00702269	1980s Rock	$16.99

00702268	1990s Rock	$24.99
00369043	Rock Songs for Kids	$14.99
00109725	Once	$14.99
00702187	Selections from O Brother Where Art Thou?	$19.99
00702178	100 Songs for Kids	$16.99
00702515	Pirates of the Caribbean	$17.99
00702125	Praise and Worship for Guitar	$14.99
00287930	Songs from *A Star Is Born, The Greatest Showman, La La Land*, and More Movie Musicals	$16.99
00702285	Southern Rock Hits	$12.99
00156420	Star Wars Music	$16.99
00121535	30 Easy Celtic Guitar Solos	$16.99
00244654	Top Hits of 2017	$14.99
00283786	Top Hits of 2018	$14.99
00302269	Top Hits of 2019	$14.99
00355779	Top Hits of 2020	$14.99
00374083	Top Hits of 2021	$16.99
00702294	Top Worship Hits	$17.99
00702255	VH1's 100 Greatest Hard Rock Songs	$34.99
00702175	VH1's 100 Greatest Songs of Rock and Roll	$34.99
00702253	Wicked	$12.99

ARTIST COLLECTIONS

00702267	AC/DC for Easy Guitar	$16.99
00156221	Adele – 25	$16.99
00396889	Adele – 30	$19.99
00702040	Best of the Allman Brothers	$16.99
00702865	J.S. Bach for Easy Guitar	$15.99
00702169	Best of The Beach Boys	$16.99
00702292	The Beatles — 1	$22.99
00125796	Best of Chuck Berry	$16.99
00702201	The Essential Black Sabbath	$15.99
00702250	blink-182 — Greatest Hits	$17.99
02501615	Zac Brown Band — The Foundation	$17.99
02501621	Zac Brown Band — You Get What You Give	$16.99
00702043	Best of Johnny Cash	$17.99
00702090	Eric Clapton's Best	$16.99
00702086	Eric Clapton — from the Album Unplugged	$17.99
00702202	The Essential Eric Clapton	$17.99
00702053	Best of Patsy Cline	$17.99
00222697	Very Best of Coldplay – 2nd Edition	$17.99
00702229	The Very Best of Creedence Clearwater Revival	$16.99
00702145	Best of Jim Croce	$16.99
00702278	Crosby, Stills & Nash	$12.99
14042809	Bob Dylan	$15.99
00702276	Fleetwood Mac — Easy Guitar Collection	$17.99
00139462	The Very Best of Grateful Dead	$16.99
00702136	Best of Merle Haggard	$16.99
00702227	Jimi Hendrix — Smash Hits	$19.99
00702288	Best of Hillsong United	$12.99
00702236	Best of Antonio Carlos Jobim	$15.99

00702245	Elton John — Greatest Hits 1970–2002	$19.99
00129855	Jack Johnson	$17.99
00702204	Robert Johnson	$16.99
00702234	Selections from Toby Keith — 35 Biggest Hits	$12.95
00702003	Kiss	$16.99
00702216	Lynyrd Skynyrd	$17.99
00702182	The Essential Bob Marley	$16.99
00146081	Maroon 5	$14.99
00121925	Bruno Mars – Unorthodox Jukebox	$12.99
00702248	Paul McCartney — All the Best	$14.99
00125484	The Best of MercyMe	$12.99
00702209	Steve Miller Band — Young Hearts (Greatest Hits)	$12.95
00124167	Jason Mraz	$15.99
00702096	Best of Nirvana	$16.99
00702211	The Offspring — Greatest Hits	$17.99
00138026	One Direction	$17.99
00702030	Best of Roy Orbison	$17.99
00702144	Best of Ozzy Osbourne	$14.99
00702279	Tom Petty	$17.99
00102911	Pink Floyd	$17.99
00702139	Elvis Country Favorites	$19.99
00702293	The Very Best of Prince	$19.99
00699415	Best of Queen for Guitar	$16.99
00109279	Best of R.E.M.	$14.99
00702208	Red Hot Chili Peppers — Greatest Hits	$17.99
00198960	The Rolling Stones	$17.99
00174793	The Very Best of Santana	$16.99
00702196	Best of Bob Seger	$16.99
00146046	Ed Sheeran	$17.99

00702252	Frank Sinatra — Nothing But the Best	$12.99
00702010	Best of Rod Stewart	$17.99
00702049	Best of George Strait	$17.99
00702259	Taylor Swift for Easy Guitar	$15.99
00359800	Taylor Swift – Easy Guitar Anthology	$24.99
00702260	Taylor Swift — Fearless	$14.99
00139727	Taylor Swift — 1989	$19.99
00115960	Taylor Swift — Red	$16.99
00253667	Taylor Swift — Reputation	$17.99
00702290	Taylor Swift — Speak Now	$16.99
00232849	Chris Tomlin Collection – 2nd Edition	$14.99
00702226	Chris Tomlin — See the Morning	$12.95
00148643	Train	$14.99
00702427	U2 — 18 Singles	$19.99
00702108	Best of Stevie Ray Vaughan	$17.99
00279005	The Who	$14.99
00702123	Best of Hank Williams	$15.99
00194548	Best of John Williams	$14.99
00702228	Neil Young — Greatest Hits	$17.99
00119133	Neil Young — Harvest	$14.99

Prices, contents and availability subject to change without notice.

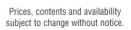

HAL•LEONARD®

Visit Hal Leonard online at **halleonard.com**

HAL•LEONARD GUITAR PLAY-ALONG

Complete song lists available online.

This series will help you play your favorite songs quickly and easily. Just follow the tab and listen to the audio to the hear how the guitar should sound, and then play along using the separate backing tracks. Audio files also include software to slow down the tempo without changing pitch. The melody and lyrics are included in the book so that you can sing or simply follow along.

INCLUDES TAB

Prices, contents, and availability subject to change without notice.

HAL•LEONARD®
www.halleonard.com

0822
173